Redemption

A story of faith, patience, and God's love and mercy for those who believe and trust in him

Karalee Ratliff

ISBN 979-8-89243-996-1 (paperback)
ISBN 979-8-89243-997-8 (digital)

Christian Faith Publishing
832 Park Avenue
Meadville, PA 16335
www.christianfaithpublishing.com

Printed in the United States of America

Introduction: A story of faith, patience, and God's love
and mercy for those who believe and trust in him.
Dedicated to my family.

Chapter One

Standing before the mirror, Alex secured and straightened his tie smartly. Today was a big day for him. Today, he would give a speech to honor his friend.

The hour was early, and he was anxious. He had practiced his speech so many times that he felt like it was right, but he also felt like he was missing something. His friend had helped him a lot over the years, and there was such a story to tell. Alex felt as though his speech was giving his friend the honor that was deserved.

As the sunlight peered through the blinds, Alex completed his task of getting dressed. He was in the suit that his friend had given him. It was his dedication suit for when he had found Jesus. It was because of his friend that Jesus was even a part of his life.

Alex had been a troubled teen. His mom had worked two or three jobs at a time to just put a decent roof over his head and food on the table. Try as she might to keep him safe, Alex had fallen into the wrong crowd. He did not know his father and had no father figure in his life. That is until he met Paul.

Paul was a business owner in the neighborhood where Alex lived. He noticed Alex trying so hard to find himself and that he was working himself into a mess of trouble. He knew that Alex's mother, Kim, was trying hard; but Alex was a teenager now and so full of himself. He had grown quite a bit taller and bulkier than his mother, and she chose to stop challenging him so much. Alex thought it was because she was afraid of him, and he was good with the idea of being in charge. No one was going to tell him what to do.

Paul was faithful Christian man and had taken an interest in Alex. As he watched Alex grow, he saw similarities in him to an army pal he had not seen in years. There were several facial parallels but nothing concrete. He knew Kim from school and knew that she was doing all that she could. So Paul decided that he would keep a watchful eye from a distance and see what he could do to help.

Occasionally, groceries would appear on their porch, or a bill would have a zero balance. All done anonymously. He knew the hardship that she was undertaking and just wanted to help. He had heard a sermon one Sunday many moons ago that there are things that we can do, things that should do, and there are things we are willing to do. He decided, then, that he was able and willing to help someone he saw in need, so he kind of adopted Alex and his mom. He did this because he could not shake the fact that there were so many nuances between Alex and his long-ago pal.

One day, Alex had decided to rob Paul's business. He walked in brazenly brandishing an old pistol and demanded the money from the cash register. Paul quietly and easily complied. Alex took the money and then demanded that Paul come from behind the counter. Carefully and cautiously, he complied with the command. Alex was now so full of himself and his power that he decided to teach Paul a lesson. As he shot a glimmer of arrogance at Paul and raised his hand with the pistol, Paul quickly secured him with a hammer lock and placed his face against the counter. He took the pistol from Alex, tossed it to the side, reached into Alex's pocket, retrieved his money, and tossed it to the counter on the other side of the register. When Alex quit fighting back, Paul released him and said, "You may leave. I will not press charges."

Confused, Alex took off out the door. Paul secured the pistol and his money then went back to work. A few days later, Alex returned to the store. Paul stood quietly behind the counter and asked, "Are you here to rob me again? Or do you think I should give you back your broken pistol so that you can scare someone else?"

Alex replied, "Why didn't you call the police?"

Paul looked at him and said, "Why? I got my money back. I wasn't hurt. Nothing was damaged. Why did I need to call the police?"

Without a response, Alex left.

Paul was in his store closing up one evening when he heard a crash in the back room. Grabbing the bat he had beneath the counter, he carefully scoped out the room. He had recently installed a bright floodlight, though at the time it did not make sense, but now he was glad he did. When he turned on the light, he could see blood on the floor, and it was growing. As he rounded the end row of boxes, he found Alex on the floor with a hole in his midsection. He had been stabbed or shot, but with the amount of blood he was losing, it would not be long until it would not matter. Tossing the bat to the side, Paul grabbed the nearest box of rags and began to pack the wound to stop the bleeding. Alex was barely conscious and whispered, "I am sorry." Paul reassured him that there was nothing to be sorry for and that everything would be all right.

Paul pulled out his cell phone and called 911. Within minutes, the ambulance was there, and they whisked Alex off to the hospital. They had asked if Paul was the boy's father, and he replied that he was not, but he knew the mother and he would go and retrieve her and meet them at the hospital.

Because Paul had adopted this family secretly, he had found out as much about them as he could without being suspicious. He knew that Kim would be at the diner working. When he got there, he tried to explain who he was but ultimately explained that she needed to come with him right now because Alex was in trouble. Thoroughly distraught, confused, and angry all in one, she went with Paul. On the way to the hospital, she bombarded him with never-ending questions of what happened, how he knew Alex, how he knew who she was and where she would be, etc. Paul drove furiously through town and pulled into the hospital. He explained that he would answer any questions she had, but all that he knew was that Alex had wandered into his storeroom hurt and needed his mom right now.

Kim got out of the vehicle and ran into the hospital. They were prepping Alex for surgery. They advised that Kim needed to sign a bunch of papers and that she would only have a minute before they would take her son. All they could tell her was that he had a big hole in his midsection, and they were doing all that they could to save him. She scribbled her name where they told her to, led her to her son, grabbed his hand, and told him everything was going to be all right; she promised. With his boyish eyes and weak voice, he whispered, "I am sorry. I love you, Mom."

With tears streaming down her face, they pulled him away from her and off to the surgical area the proceeded. One nurse put her arm around Kim and escorted her to a private waiting room. She explained that if she wanted to contact anyone in the family, it might be a good idea to do so. Kim looked at the nurse and told her, "There is no family. I am all he has. He is all I have. Please save him."

The nurse reassured her that they had their best team on the table, and they would do everything they could. As the nurse was leaving the room, she explained to Kim that there were pastors on call if she wanted to speak to them. That they could have one here to the hospital really soon. Kim, wiping her tears and trying to catch her breath, said thank-you; but she was going to be all right. She just needed to be alone. When the nurse opened the door to leave, Paul was standing there. The nurse asked if she could help him, and Paul replied that he was there to support Kim. Looking at Kim for approval, the nurse hesitated in letting Paul in. Kim nodded her head, Paul entered, and the nurse left, closing the door slowly.

"You said that you would answer all my questions? Well, I seem to have a lot of time on my hands right now, so will you?" Kim said with a firm jaw and wiping her tears away.

"Yes, ma'am. I am man of my word. Ask away," Paul replied.

"Who are you, for starters?"

"My name is Paul Smith. I run a little shop over on 32nd Street."

"Okay, Paul Smith from 32nd Street, who are you? How do you know Alex? Why is he injured? How did you know how and where to find me?"

"I am a man of my word. I will tell you everything. But please listen to everything I have to say. Then if you want me to leave, I will. I will give you no trouble. Will you agree?"

"I don't have much choice now do I? That is if I want any answers." Kim was beginning to get defensive in her demeanor.

"As I said, I am Paul Smith. I run a small shop over on 32nd Street. I was born and raised right here. I joined the army right out of high school and moved home when my enlistment was over."

"Okay…what does…"

"I asked you to let me tell you everything."

"Continue then."

"I joined the army and then moved home after my contract was over. I had several jobs before I decided to try my hand at my shop. I remember you and Alex moving into the neighborhood and thinking, 'Another single mom, great.' But over the course of the next days, weeks, and months, I noticed that you were not just another single mom. You were a *single mom*, meaning you were trying to make a difference for your son. I admired that. I have watched as Alex has grown up and how difficult it is for you and how tired you must feel. One day, I passed you in the grocery store, and I thought how much Alex looked like an old battle buddy of mine. But I had not spoken to that buddy in many years, so I brushed it off as coincidence. After that, I could not shake you two. Then one day in church, the pastor talked about things that we can do, should do, and will do. So from a distance, I tried to help you as much as I could. I left you food when I thought it might be needed. I paid a couple of your bills anonymously to help out. I did not want to intrude, but it felt like God was leading me to help, and being a faithful follower, I dare not say no. I know this all seems weird and creepy. I get it. But there is more."

Kim sat there with a dumbfounded look upon her face. She recalled the times she had gone to pay the past due bills, and they had zero balances. She recalled the times that she came home, and Alex was eating a snack or sandwich, and she knew that she had not been shopping, that he told her that there was food on the porch when he got home from school. Stoic and in shock, she listened to Paul explain himself.

"One day not too long ago, Alex came into my shop with a pistol and robbed me. He was on a serious power trip and tried to teach me lesson. I disarmed him, got my money back, and told him I would not press charges. To leave. A few days later, he returned to ask me why. I explained that no one was hurt, I got my money back so no harm no foul. He left. I had not seen him for several days when I found him tonight in my back storage room, bleeding. As I packed his wound, he whispered he was sorry. I assume it was for his robbery attempt, but I do not know."

"Why didn't you call the police when robbed you? No one just lets bad people go like that."

"Alex is not a bad kid. He is just trying to find his way. He did not succeed in robbing me or assaulting me. There was no damage except to his ego. I figured that was enough of a punishment."

"I am thankful you were there to help him."

"Do you want me to leave, or may I stay here with you and wait for Alex?"

"I would like you to stay. I don't know why, but I have a good feeling about you. I should be scared as hell, but there is something about you. Please stay."

The two sat in silence and talked sporadically about the weather, the shop, her jobs, and trivial nonsense to pass the time. It seemed like an eternity had passed and still no word from the hospital staff. Paul offered to fetch them a bite or some coffee. Though she was not particularly hungry, she agreed. She playfully asked if he knew what she liked, he replied, "Hot and edible?"

With a slight smile, she said, "You really did your homework on me."

Paul left and Kim was alone again. Where did this guy come from? He seems like a nice guy, but who does this kind of thing today? Her mind was racing with all the negative possibilities, and maybe she should get away from him as quickly as possible. But he had saved her son's life, at least for now, how could she not see that. Then her mind wondered if Paul was actually the assailant and was putting on a front.

When Paul returned, Kim tried to distance herself emotionally to see if she could read Paul. Paul caught on and reassured her that he did not hurt Alex.

As they sat together and ate their sandwiches, Kim began to ask about Paul's past. What he saw in Alex that made him become so interested. Paul tried to explain that he had this very brave pal in the army who did more tours than he had. He had been on several deployments, and there were just so many similarities. He realized that the odds of Alex and him being related were like nil, but for him, he felt like it was close enough for government work. Then when the sermon was taught about what to do, he decided why not. Even if he isn't Alex's father, this family needs help. "So I helped."

"Where is your family?" Kim inquired.

"My wife and I split up after we lost—" Paul stopped and took another bite of his sandwich.

"I am sorry. I am prying. It is not my business."

"We lost our son to cancer when he was very young. The devastation it caused was more than either of us could handle. We started taking it out on each other, and then we just quit. After we split, I went through a rough spell and a pastor friend of mine invited me to church. Reluctantly, I went, and I have been going ever since. My wife—ex-wife—and I are still on speaking terms, but it is difficult. We burnt a lot of bridges in our grief. Not sure they will ever be mended."

"I am sorry."

The door opened and the doctor walked in. "Ms. Harrison? I am Dr. Phillips. I operated on your son."

Kim turned her attention to the doctor and asked, "How is he?"

"Ma'am, your son took a sizable thrust from a knife to his abdomen area. Whoever stabbed him meant for him to not live. They intentionally thrusted and twisted repeatedly to do maximum damage. However, whoever packed the wound saved his life. It took quite a bit of work, but we have him sewn back together. It is going to be a long road of physical therapy, but I believe that he will make a full recovery."

Kim collapsed into Paul's arms weeping tears of relief. Paul wrapped his arms around her and pulled her close as he whispered, "Thank you, Jesus."

"When can we see him, Doc?" Paul asked.

"He is in recovery now. He will be there a few more hours, I would suggest that you go home and get some rest, he will be here in the morning. He needs his rest right now."

"Sir, can I please just see my son? I promise not to disturb him. I just need to see my son," Kim pleaded.

"Five minutes. Nurse, take Ms. Harrison to see her son. Five minutes."

"Yes, Doctor."

Chapter Two

"You look so handsome. You are going to give a great speech today. Are you nervous?"

"Mom, really?" Alex looked at Kim with a snarky but loving grin. "Do I look nervous?" he replied with an arrogant tone.

Giggling, she stated that he looked like he was very nervous. As Alex continued to prepare for the events of the day, Kim recognized just how much Alex looked like his father. She could not unsee what was standing before her. It had not been a big issue before, but now, with all that has happened, and in this moment, Kim wished that she knew where Alex's father was and how he was doing. Rather than linger in moments of the unknown, Kim decided to tease her son some more. The two playfully jabbed at each other all the way to the banquet hall.

Today was the day that the town recognized Paul for his heroics in saving Alex's life. It had been five years since the incident, several things had happened since then, but when the story of Paul's compassion and mentorship was heard, it was a unanimous decision for him to be recognized as the Good Samaritan of the year.

At the hall, Alex and Kim mingled with several of the committee who had selected Paul. Friends from the diner were there. Church members were there. In addition to reporters for both the newspaper and television. Upon seeing the cameras, Alex tugged at his mom's arm and pulled her aside. "Cameras?" he whispered with a bit of fear in his voice. Placing her arm around his, taking her other hand and holding his hands, she reassured him that he was going to be fantastic. "Just speak from your heart and speak to Paul. Ignore everything and everyone else. This is just you telling Paul how you feel. That is all." With a hesitant sigh, Alex's demeanor settled a bit.

The hall was filling up. There were at least two hundred people here. Kim could see the anxiousness building again in Alex and reassured him yet again. When Alex saw Paul, he bolted right up to him and asked, "So you ready for this roast old man?" with a huge smile on his face.

Paul laughed and said, "Bring it, little boy, show me what you got." Then the two embraced and Kim laughed at how much they seemed like father and son. And in a way, they were. Paul was definitely the father figure Alex needed, and Alex was the son that Paul needed.

"Good afternoon, everyone. I would like to thank you all for attending this wonderful recognition of a truly amazing man. As the committee heard about how this man"—the emcee directed his hand toward Paul—"has been such an influence in the community and to this family in particular, we could not have all agreed more in who should receive this year's award. We have several speakers to speak on his behalf so please join us in recognizing our Good Samaritan of the Year…Paul Smith."

The crowd stood, and the hall erupted in a thunder of clapping and whistles. Many of the audience knew Paul and all knew he was good man. But none of them knew about his encounter with Alex and his family, less one, his pastor. Tom was the only one Paul had confided in because he truly believed he was to store up his treasures in heaven and not on earth, but on a couple of occasions, Paul had to seek Tom's advice on how to proceed.

The first speaker was Paul's ex-wife, Melony. When they called her name to begin, Paul was in shock. He had no idea, except for Alex, who was on the docket to speak. When she took the stand and explained how she knew Paul, there was a "silence" in the room. Normally you do not have exes on the good side. She proceeded to tell of the man she met so many years ago who had stolen her heart. They married while he was still in service, and when his tour was up, he knew he wanted to be total family man. She regaled their life together as a fairy tale in proportion that ended tragically. She expressed the good times and ultimately the demise of their marriage. She had stated that when word of Paul's service in the community became public, she was not surprised. She knew that Paul was an amazing man and that he was destined to do amazing things.

As she continued her speech, Paul's eyes filled with tears of love and peace over their relationship. He was watching the woman that had stolen his heart pour out her soul to a large group of people in praise over a man who had broken her heart, yet she still loved him. Paul could feel her emotions and passion for their life together and apart. When she stated that she knew that God had a plan for him, he could contain his tears no more. For she had walked away from God after their son's death and to hear that meant that she had, at least, began reconciling her faith again.

At the end of her speech, there was not a dry eye. Every man and woman, including Alex and Kim, were flooding the floors. Paul rose and approached Melony, they each grabbed the other and embraced as the thunderous approval from the audience engulfed the hall.

Alex leaned over to Kim and said, "Mom, I am so nervous. I don't know how I am going to do this."

Kim whispered back in her bestest, loving-mom reassuring tone, "Honey, you got this. Think about how hard it was for her to stand before this crowd and reveal her heart. You got this. Just speak the truth." She pulled Alex close and wiped the tears from his face.

The emcee, still drying her eyes, approached the mike to announce the next speaker. "I apologize if my voice is broken. I knew this man was worthy, but this first encounter to better understanding him has really solidified my vote in this decision and I cannot wait to hear more about this amazing man." She paused and then introduced the next speaker, "Tom, Paul's pastor."

"Good afternoon to everyone. I am so blessed to be a part of this dedication to this fine man. Several years ago, I had the pleasure of meeting him at a random event and we began talking about... you know, I am not even sure what we were talking about exactly. However, I do recall it turning into a debate that became slightly heated and ended in us in a mud pit defended each other. It was an odd day."

As Tom recalled their meeting, Paul was laughing as he relived that day. It was that day that changed Paul's life and his perspective on life. At the time, Paul had given up on God and was in a very dark arena. When he met Tom, it was like a light switch had been turned on in his heart. Paul could hear the debate as if it were yesterday; but he, too, could not remember how it got started. However, he did totally recall how it ended, he and Tom covered in mud laughing hysterically.

"Let me embellish—no, that is probably not the right word, bear with me, I am just a pastor. I have trouble finding the right words to speak and talking in front of crowds scare me." The crowd erupted with laughter. "This man, Paul Smith, is one of the finest I have ever met. After that mud bath, I invited him to my church to which he promptly gave me 'are you nuts?' look. I bated him with a solid lure, and the next Sunday, he was there and has been there every Sunday since. He has since given his life back to Jesus and, as this award indicates, has served our Father in heaven well. Paul did not tell me of his journey until such a time where he felt like he may be crossing boundaries. He did not want dishonor God but felt like he was supposed to do more. As he confided in me all that he had taken on, we prayed together for guidance. Though an answer was not revealed right then, we both were texted that night at 3:00 a.m. and texted the other. It was the oddest thing. We texted and sent the same answer to each other at exactly the same time. As my text sent, his appeared. Now if that is not God, don't know how to explain it." Tom continued to raise Paul and his service up and acknowledge his approval, as such, for Paul to receive this award. At the end of his speech, Tom challenged Paul to the sand box at the church for a rematch. Paul politely declined and embraced his friend.

Three more speakers were called. All of them gave similar accounts of God-driven encounters with Paul. All were detailed in explanation and in gratefulness. The emcee explained that they had one more remarkable story to tell but wanted to take a five-minute break so that the last speaker could prepare.

Paul approached Alex and asked, "Prepare?"

Alex smiled and said, "You are a nosey one, aren't you? Don't you trust me?"

Paul quickly responded, "not anymore." The two laughed, and Alex began to set up for his speech.

The five-minute intermission turned into fifteen because of technical difficulties, but as everyone reassembled in the hall, there was a large screen on a platform to the left of the stage and a projector.

The emcee introduced Alex and Kim took the mike. A little confused, the emcee stepped aside, this was not disclosed prior to the banquet so it caught them a little off guard.

"My name is Kim Harrison. Not Alex. Alex is my son. He asked me to start you all off with a brief description from my point of view. I was not exactly inclined to do so, but when he explained why, I could not say no. We have planned this from the time we heard that our recommendation for Paul to be recognized for the wonderful man that he is and with the help of his ex-wife, we have prepared a special presentation to honor this man."

Paul's face went blank. What had Alex, Kim, and Mel concocted? The light's dimmed, and Alex began to play on his keyboard a remembrance melody. The projector turned on, and a series of screens appeared. The first explained the gratitude that Alex had for Paul and that without Paul, Alex would not be who he is today. While Alex played, a series of photos began to play on the screen. Old high school photos of Paul in his fantastic seventies plaid bell bottoms and his football uniform. Following with his enlistment photo, a few from when he was in the army to his wedding photo. The presentation continued with him holding his son, Carter, and the look of pure love in his eyes. Next came the devastating loss and the pictures of Paul's demeanor changed dramatically. The photos then changed to random pictures of Paul's new shop and simple things he had done with the church. A lot of the photos Paul recognized and remembered, but there were a few that he did not know existed. Throughout this presentation, Melony and Tom explained the different occasions. When they came to the last church photo, Alex began to talk. The slideshow moved to a picture of Christ.

"Ladies and gentlemen, my name is Alex Harrison. No, that is not my picture up there. That man we are showing you is the man who sent Mr. Paul into my life." A light chuckle fell about the room. The slideshow switched to Alex's boyhood.

"These photos are of me when I was little. My mom, Kim, is the hot momma in these photos. She is currently single and is a great catch." The crowd laughed. "The onery little tike is me. She worked all the time to make sure that I had food to eat and clothes on my back. I never knew my dad, and to this day, I do not know the story behind him not being in my life. But that does not matter. Because you see, Jesus brought this man [a photo of Paul appeared] into my life to knock some sense into me. [The photo array switched back to Alex as a seventeen-year-old who was angry at the world.] At the time of this photograph, I was very much a 'man' on a mission to sink myself, and I did not realize it. I was the big guy on campus. My mom quit trying to make me do what I did not want to do. I always thought it was because she knew I could overpower her, but that was not the case. It was because…though we didn't know it at the time…it was because God was sending us our angel. On May 12, I entered Paul's shop with a gun and robbed him. I didn't bother to cover my face because I was sure I was scary enough like in the movies that I could intimidate him to stay quiet. When I entered his shop brandishing my gun, he politely and quietly complied with my demands. I was so sure that I was the real McCoy that I ordered him from behind the counter so I could give him a beat down. You know, show my power. I can tell you this: That was the moment in life that I will never forget. I do not know how, but in a split second, I was robbed of my bounty, my weaponry, and my pride in one fell swoop. Then I was sent packing. Sent packing without a police escort or new bracelets. That was even more humiliating."

Paul sat and listened intently to Alex's recollection of that day's events. Paul studied the crowd and watched their reactions as Alex spoke. He could read several different sets of eyes, but the atmosphere was amazing.

"I returned to his shop a few weeks later to ask why he did not call the cops on me that day. In a nutshell, he explained grace and mercy without stating grace and mercy. It did not make sense to me at the time. A little while later, I found myself in a battle with some people that I thought I was better than and could overpower with my 'manliness' and found myself bleeding in short order. I was only a couple blocks from Paul's shop and did not know then but was compelled to go to Paul." There was silence in the crowd. "In short order, Paul had me fixed up and on my way to the hospital. He found my mom and took her to the hospital also. I do not know how he knew but he did. Since that day, Paul has been by my side in my recovery and my life with Jesus. He has been a father figure and a mentor."

Alex paused with his speech. He had to compose himself because the next slides were of him in the hospital; and those, he knew, were difficult for his mom to see. They took them so that they could always have reference to where Alex had been and how far that he had come. However, these were painful memories.

The projector switched, and it was Alex in the hospital bed hooked up to all kinds of machines. He took a breath and continued.

"This man is more than a hero. He is more than a good Samaritan. In my opinion, he is an angel. Jesus sent him to me and my mom to save me from myself and provide a support that my mom has never had, a true friend."

As the last of the slides played, the lights came on. Alex quit playing his keyboard and was now at the podium.

"Ladies and gentlemen, they say a picture is worth a thousand words. I showed you at least a hundred pictures and with simple math that is at least a hundred thousand words. In just the photos, add to that the commentary, we are well past one million, and we are not even through the surface of what or who this man is. Especially to me. He was with me and mom before we knew him. He was with me even though I disrespected him. He was with me and mom throughout my recovery. He was—is—with me and Mom as we begin our journeys with Jesus. I would not be here today, on many levels, if it were not for this magnificent man. Any other person would have written me off as a lost cause. This man, Paul Smith, he is one of a kind. He is a true follower of Jesus. He saw something in me that only my mom saw and could not get me to see."

Paul was in full-fledged sobs. Kim was constantly wiping the tears away. Alex took some tissue and cleaned his face then turned to face Paul directly. "Mr. Paul, words cannot express my gratitude and love that I have for you. You saved my life. You are and forever will be…my dad."

At this, Paul stood, and with a hearty embrace, he and Alex hugged. The crowd rose in applause and love. "I love you too, son."

Paul whispered, "Thank you. You saved me as well."

As the afternoon came to a close, Paul had accepted the award with a mess of a face from the love and outpouring of affection shown to him. He was humbled by the award, the speeches, and love. It was almost more than he could handle.

Chapter Three

Paul was sitting in his easy chair, reflecting on the banquet. He really wished his brother could have been there. Unfortunately, due to the short notice, travel plans could not be made in time. His brother offered to come to celebrate with a better planned visit, but Paul told him the fact that he wanted to come was good enough for him. They had spoken right after the ceremony, and Paul sent him a picture of the plaque. His brother expressed how proud he was and that he would be visiting very soon.

Knock, knock.

Paul got up from his chair to answer the door. "Good evening, sir, can I interest you in a piece of pie?"

"*Tim!*" Paul exclaimed. "Mary."

"What are you two doing here?"

"Well, brother, I said I could not make the ceremony because there were no flights, then you cut me off and said it was all right. I tried to tell you that we could come a bit later, but then you cut me off again. So…*surprise!*"

With excitement, bewilderment, and exhausting joy and happiness, Paul grabbed them both and locked them into a welcoming bear hug. Laughing and gasping for air, Mary and Tim asked to be released from this bondage.

The three moved to the front room and took a seat. Paul still reeling over their appearance, "So did you fly or drive?"

Mary explained that they flew into the local airport…two hours away. Said that she had happened upon some red-eye priced tickets, and they hopped on it. She apologized for them not being able to town in time for the ceremony. "Mary, my love, if you ever decide to leave this clod brother of mine, I have lots of room right here."

"Listen here, you troll of a brother, I know what we fed you through the slats of the porch, keep away from my princess."

"See, that is the problem. You think she is a princess when she is indeed a queen." Paul rose and then bowed to her majesty. Mary just shook her head and laughed. Tim jumped up and slammed into Paul, driving him over the coffee table and onto the couch. Mary was able to maneuver out of the way just in time as the two wanting-to-be-teenage boys wrestled around the furniture laughing. As they ultimately pinned themselves between the table and the sofa, once they caught their breath from laughing so hard and much, they had to beg the princess queen for some assistance. Mary was congenial to obliged but not until she got some good blackmail shots of this predicament for the kids when they got home.

They decided to move the discussion into the kitchen and sit like grown-ups at the table. Paul and Tim continued the brotherly barbs. Mary piped in every so often to either calm the situation or egg them on.

"Can I get either of you a drink or something to eat?" Paul inquired when he finally realized that he was not being very host like.

"Well, little brother, In honor of this great achievement, like you needed another one to hold over my head…" Tim started with a smirky smile.

"Tim, behave." Mary pulled out her mom tone in playful manner.

"In honor of this great achievement, I would like to take you out for dinner. But not tonight. It is late, and Mary and I need to get back to the hotel and get some rest. She is not as young as she used to be and needs her beauty sleep."

"TIMOTHY…YOU WILL THINK BEAUTY REST/SLEEP." Mary turned to him and slugged his arm.

The three of them hugged again. Paul offered them a place, but Tim said that Mary's snoring would keep them both awake all night. That he would suffer for them both, and they would see him in the morning once she made herself presentable. Mary slugged Tim again, and they all hugged. A time was set for them to meet for breakfast at the local restaurant. Tim and Mary said their goodbyes and left for the hotel.

"Tim, why has it been so long since we have come to see Paul? Do you recall if there was a reason?" Mary asked once they were in the car.

"I am not sure. I think just everything that has happened in the last couple of years, ya know. I don't think there was a reason. I think we just got busy."

"That could be. I don't want us to go this long again. We need to be closer as a family. I wonder if we could set up a family gathering somehow. The only problem is that we are all spread out. I just don't want the next time we see each other to be because of someone passing away. Seeing him tonight brought back fond memories of when we all used to barbecue before." Mary paused. "Before the…before Carter got sick, and then we moved away." Tim reached over and put his hand on hers. "I always thought that our kids would grow up together somehow and be best friends."

Tim pulled into the hotel. After they got into the room, Tim pulled Mary close. "Mary, my love, I know. I thought the same thing. But after Carter died, it was not a good place for us to be. That is why we moved closer to Mom. That way we could take care of her. We tried to get Paul and Melony to come with us. But they were stuck here and then they had no support. I feel bad, but…it looks like it all worked out for them."

The two of them prepared for bed and curled up next to each other for the night.

Ring, buzz. Ring, buzz. Ring, buzz.

"What is that?" Tim rolled over and saw that his cell phone was going off. Wiping the sleep from his eyes, he noticed a text message from Colton. He then noticed that the time was 5:00 a.m. As his eyes began to focus, Mary asked, "What is going on?"

Tim replied, "I don't know I have a text from Colton."

"Is there something wrong?"

"Mary, I don't know, I am trying to find out. Hold on."

Tim wiped the sleep from his eyes, sat up in bed, and focused on the brightness of the phone. Once he was able to see straightly, he read, "I just wanted to inform you that there has been an issue with your home. I am sorry that you entrusted me with this beautiful property, but there has been a situation. I have notified Janie and Jon. They will be here today to help me with the evictions, but I felt it necessary to let you know that your property has been overran with turds."

Tim had been reading aloud the text message to Mary so as to not have to repeat himself. When he completed the text, he and Mary agreed that the payback was going to be brutal.

They both decided that 5:00 a.m. was too early to get up and cozied back down for a couple more hours of sleep. Breakfast was not until nine.

The alarm clock went off promptly at 7:00 a.m. Paul was up and ready to rock and roll. He had not felt this alive in a very long time. Yesterday was over the top with the award, the speeches, Melony's testimony, Alex's dedication, then Tim and Mary arriving. It was a beautiful dream that he did not want to wake up from.

He jumped into the shower, and as the water pelted his body, he felt stinging and stiffness. *Bet I probably should not wrestle with Tim again today.* He giggled. *Unless of course he starts it ya know,* Paul thought. He finished his shower and found the best worst clothes to wear. He knew that Tim had something up his sleeve; he just was not sure what it was. So he needed to be prepared.

Over at the hotel, Tim and Mary grabbed their showers. Mary had taken hers last, and when she exited the bathroom, Tim was dressed in the most god-awful outfit she had ever seen. "What do you think you are doing?" she exclaimed.

"This is my 'gonna git my brother outfit,'" Tim proclaimed proudly. Mary tried to change his mind then realized that she was up against a mountain of fortified toddlers, and she was not going to make any progress. She then changed her mind as to what to wear, but only slightly because she felt like someone should be a grown-up. However, she needed to be prepared for any spillage that might occur.

The three arrived in near synchronous time. Paul proudly exited his vehicle in green, cut-off pants with bright orange suspenders, a Spam man tank top, diabetic socks up to his knees and…to top it off, a bow tie. Tim, not to be outdone, got out in his bright orange and black striped leggings, torn up yellow shorts, a purple frill crop top tied up like Daisy Duke, and a propellered beanie cap. As the two brothers paraded their fashion sense for the world to see, Mary shot several snapshots and sent them to the kids so they could see what happens when this two get together. They would not have believed her otherwise.

With great dignified prowess, the two men sauntered into the restaurant and found a table in the middle of the establishment. They wanted to make sure everyone could see. Mary just followed and laughed at their antics. Throughout the meal, the boys created quite the show. Many people stopped to ask Paul if he was feeling all right. Did he hit the sauce after the banquet? Was he having a breakdown? And various questions of that nature. No one had ever seen this side of Paul. They only knew the kindhearted shop owner, not the silly side.

Chapter Four

"I swear, I cannot take you two anywhere. Are you twelve again or what?" Mary claimed as she took the condiments away from the two boys. Paul and Tim had the beginnings of a ketchup-mustard war looming, and though their outfits might benefit from the additional makeup, Mary did not want to get caught in the crossfire; after all, she was the normal one today.

The two men continued their playful antics much to the amusement of the restaurant. Mary played referee when it appeared that something might be damaged, and the cost of the meal would increase exponentially. The two men were definitely in their boyish element this morning. It did Mary's heart good to see the brothers enjoying each other. It had been a very long time since she had seen such a jovial encounter of this magnitude.

"Paul?" came a voice that stopped Paul in mid-antic. "Paul? Is that really you?" Paul turned around, and with a hearty belt of laughter, Tim could read his brother's embarrassed face tenfold.

Alex and Kim had entered the diner for lunch and walked in on the festivities. Alex always felt there was another side to Paul, but this was not the direction he was thinking, and he loved it. Kim looked at Mary with a bewildered look to which Mary replied with a shrugged-shoulders, what-can-you-do kind of look. Mary then invited the two to join the festivities and enjoy the brotherly love. Alex looked at his mom with delight and eagerness to join the table. Paul, already embarrassed, asked that they join them—the more, the merrier. By now, Tim was beside himself with gut-wrenching laughter at Paul's embarrassment, pulled two chairs from a nearby table, and helped to make room for them. Kim and Alex sat down, and Tim took the opportunity to further humiliate his brother. Paul tried to straighten up, but Tim was not having it, and soon, Paul was back at it, full force.

By the time the food came, everyone had eaten, and the mess was beyond anyone's comprehension; the staff and the patrons in the diner were in full-blown laughter and enjoying the antics of two very loving brothers. Mary paid the bill for the food of everyone, left a sizable tip for their embellishment of the "children," and an extra amount to cover any extra cleaning costs that might come up due to her "children." The diner staff thanked her not only for her tips but also for her enthusiasm and entertainment for the morning.

As they were standing outside the diner, Tim looked at Mary and said, "I think Ayla should have an all-in out food fight day in the diner at home. Paul could come visit, and we could start it off with a bang. What do you think?"

Shaking her head, Mary replied, "Tim, get the towel out of the backseat and clean yourself off before getting in the rental."

With a smirk of defiance, Tim replied, "Yes, ma'am."

Turning her attention to Kim and Alex, Mary offered, "We are having a cookout this evening in honor of Paul's award. Would you like to join us? I cannot promise the same entertainment, but I cannot promise there won't be entertainment either. These two are a bit on the bonkers side it appears and who knows what will happen. It is not going to be anything fancy, burgers and 'dogs and laughter. Would you come? I would like to get to know the people that honored Paul."

Kim and Alex graciously agreed to come and offered to bring some chips and drinks.

"Mom, can you believe that Paul was acting like that?" Alex said in the car. "That was hilarious. I didn't think old people knew how to be like that."

"I mean he is cool and all, but...that was really awesome. I think you would have busted me for sure if I had done any of that."

With a quick mom smile, Kim replied, "You bet I would. But not for any other reason than I would have to pay for any damages and Paul is a grown man able to pay for his own choices." The two laughed all the way to the house.

Once at the hotel, Mary and Tim prepared for a trip to the store to pick up the party supplies.

"Mary, thank you," Tim commented.

"You are welcome, my dear. It was great to see you two acting like kids again. I am just glad you didn't do anything 'too' bad that we could not cover." The two of them giggled. Tim changed his clothes, and they headed off to the store.

In the car, Tim asked Mary, "Did you notice anything about Kim and Alex?"

Mary answered, "What do you mean?"

"I don't know, there was just something about them that felt familiar. Maybe I was just caught in the moment of fun and games."

Later that evening, Mary and Tim arrived at Paul's. He had pulled his old-fashioned charcoal grill from the dark recesses of his garage, dusted it off, cleaned the grill itself, and now had a pretty large flame towering off the bowl of charcoal. Paul had changed into normal adult clothes. Kim and Alex arrived, and everyone began to set up the picnic table and lawn chairs. Alex jumped to help Paul with the grill and Tim took his brotherly stance as boss overlord.

The evening took off with flying colors. There were lots of laughs, jabs, stories of the old days and explanations of how Paul and Alex became pals. When Mary inquired about Alex's father, the mood sobered a bit and Kim replied, "I have not seen nor heard from him since the night I conceived Alex. It was a night of passion and did not think of him until I found I was with child. By then he had long gone, and I only knew what he told me his first name was. I hold no hard feelings for or against him, but Alex is and has been my world."

"If I am not being too presumptuous, what was his name? I am only curious. If I am pressing, I apologize," Mary stated. Kim took a drink of her tea and said, "You are fine. His name was Cole. At least that is what I remember. I was pretty toasted that night. His name could have been nightingale, for all I know." Kim attempted to deflect the question and situation with a touch of humor.

Moving on from this topic, the group engaged in a multitude of slams, jabs, and pranks well into the night. By the end of the party, half of the neighborhood had stopped by to enjoy a side they had never encountered with Paul before.

While they were cleaning up, Kim thanked Paul, Mary, and Tim for inviting them to the barbecue. It was the most fun she had had in a very long time. She and Alex packed up in their car and left. Tim and Paul secured the chairs and table in the garage. Mary gave Paul a huge hug and kiss on the cheek and said that they would see him in the morning for coffee. Tim and Paul did some awkward dance and attempted chest bump then embraced like loving brothers.

After Mary and Tim had left, Paul sat on his couch and sighed. He thanked God for the days before and the day he was in. He thanked him for bringing Tim and Mary to visit. He thanked him for all the blessings and fell asleep right there on the sofa.

Chapter Five

"Mary, my love," Tim began, "will you stay back in the hotel tomorrow? I would like to go talk to Paul alone. We had fun today, but I really have a feeling that I need to talk to him alone. Brother to brother. I am not sure why. But the feeling is strong, and I have not felt this way since Colton came into our lives. That was a few years ago and…" Tim paused, took a deep breath, then looked intently into Mary's eyes.

Mary, who had been praying all day on a way to introduce the idea of tomorrow's visit to be just the brothers, wiped a tear from her eyes, and exclaimed that she agreed that tomorrow should just be Tim and Paul. Mary said that she had felt an urgency for connection between the two of them shortly after they landed. At first, she thought it was just the jitters of it being so long since they had been together, but after the restaurant and the barbecue, she knew that the two of them needed to talk…without a hovering old hen cackling side comments. Mary further told Tim that she knew that there was another reason that they had come to see Paul. She just did not know exactly why. She thought, well maybe it had to do with his young friend, but she was not sure. God had not revealed that to her yet. She let Tim know that she would make good use of her time, and if they were inclined, then the three could have dinner together; if not, she would forage for something edible at a nearby diner.

The two giggled at the idea of Mary making good use of her time and foraging. Two things that totally contracted her. First, she had no problems staying time-oriented. Second, she is more likely to tell the diner people how to prepare it correctly—with a smile, of course.

Mary and Tim said their respective prayers and then laid down together, huddled in each's arms. "Mary, I love you." Tim sighed as he drifted off to sleep. "I love you too, Tim." The two fell asleep in the peaceful love of God's presence in their room, their relationship to each other and their relationship with him. Since his accident, their bond has never been stronger. Mary was in heaven.

You know what you are going to find over at your brother's right. He has taken an interest in a young boy who is clearly mine. I have had that boy since the day he was born. I even got your brother—haha!—right after I "took" his son. Nothing you can say or do will change that. You may have escaped my grasp, but you—HA…YOU cannot get these two. They are mine.

Tim's dreams were repeated versions of the enemy trying to psych him out. Tim had become accustomed to hearing this voice and tuning him out. He knew that it was just desperate attempts to play mind games with him. When Tim awoke in the morning, Mary was still sound asleep. Tim made his way to the lobby for a cup of coffee and a breath of fresh air in the front porch area of the hotel.

The air was a bit cooler than Tim would have liked, but he adapted with his coffee. Sitting beneath the oak tree in front of the hotel, Tim prayed, "Lord, I come to you simply as me. I do not have fancy words. I do not have fancy ideas. I do not know the scriptures like I should. But I know you can hear me. Thank you for bringing me here to my brother. I do not know exactly why, but I know you wanted me here. I know that young Alex has something to do with it as well. I do not understand what exactly is going on. What it is that you want from me. But I am here. It is a might chilly here this morning, Lord, could you chill out on that breeze? It is cooling my coffee too fast. Lord, you found me when I was lost. You brought me a grandson who guided me to you. You gave me a childlike spirit to play with the kids. You softened my heart of adulthood and made me fun again. Thank you. Then, Lord, I know I don't have to replay the scenes, but you brought me Colton. I am not a very good example of a witness, yet you have used me to help others." Tim took a few minutes to watch the sunrise. The wind calmed down and the temperature warmed slightly with the lack of breeze. "Thank you, Lord.

You have pulled me from the fiery pits and saved me. I am asking you now that you give me the knowledge that I need to talk to Paul. I know that he has come home to you. I read that in his emails. But something is missing. I am not sure what. What does Alex have to do with it all? Father, help me to understand your message. Help me to deliver your love. Help me to help Paul. Help me to be your servant."

Tim finished off his coffee and returned to the lobby for a second round. Inside he found Mary sitting at a table. "Honey, you all right?" Mary turned to Tim and told him that she had a weird dream most of the night and that she just could not sleep anymore. Tim looked at her and said, "I had the same dream. I don't have to know the details. I know we had the same dream. It was about Paul and Alex, wasn't it?"

"Yes." Mary looked at Tim then said, "Tim, we are here for a reason, and we are doing something that is necessary. I don't know what, but…"

Placing his arms around his beautiful wife, Tim said, "Yes, we are. I love you."

The two sat quietly in the hotel lobby drinking their coffee and enjoying the sunrise through the picturesque windows. It was a beautiful sight over the hillside.

Chapter Six

"Timmy, my lad, where is that beautiful wife of yours? I do wish to dazzle her away from you and Trollip through the fairy dust land of love and lust." Paul greeted Tim from his front porch.

"Paul, she said that she could not handle us anymore together. Two days of the two of us, she said it was worse than taking all the kids to the toy store. She is taking a break."

"Coffee?"

"Well, of course."

"It is in the house, you are big boy. You can get it." Paul giggled as he sipped his hot coffee.

Tim playfully shoved his shoulder as he passed and posed to pounce. Paul gave the brotherly gaze of "Please do" but in his mind saying, "Please don't." Tim went into the kitchen to find a Mickey Mouse tumbler on the counter for him. Laughter erupted. Though he did like Mickey Mouse, he was a big boy and went on the search for a man cup.

What do you expect to accomplish here? Paul is just putting on an act…an act that I have told him to do because he is mine. He is still an old, drunken womanizer. He is mine. You cannot have him.

As he poured his coffee, the enemy began to fill Tim's head with darkened thoughts. Tim remembered the dark time after Carter died and how Paul had jumped into a bottle. Many rumors had circulated about him and various women. None of the rumors were mentioned in the divorce, and no one had spoken of them to the best of his knowledge. Tim continued to prepare his coffee and replied to the voice, "You are right, he is a drunk. He is drunk on Jesus. And that sucks for you. Nice try."

Tim walked out onto the porch and sat down next to Paul. Brotherly jabs and reminiscing commenced. The two spoke of every territory under the sun. Then when the insignificant topics had all been breached, they looked at each other and simultaneously asked the other, "How have you truly been?"

A light chuckle came, and then they both explained, "You first." Again, another chuckle. Followed by "Stop it" by both. Laughter was inevitable. The men took a second to regroup, when Paul slightly glanced at Tim and Tim at Paul. Now it was a competition to see who would win. A few minutes passed, and Tim asked sincerely, "Paul, how have you been? For real?"

Paul gave him a mischievous smile but then answered, "It has been rough. When Carter died, I died. Melony and I were fighting each other all the time, and it were just too much. For both of us. So we agreed to separate…permanently. She was and is the only one for me, but the pain was just too great. As far as I know, there is no one else with her, but I do not think that we will ever be (us) again. Then when I was at my lowest, I met Tom. He did not come as a 'preacher' but just some dude. Then watching Alex grow up, I imagined Carter. What Carter would have been like. They would be about the same age. He looks a lot like the guy I served with and maybe that is why I took a shine to him. I have my shop. It is doing well. I am no Rockefeller, but it pays my bills, and I am happy." Paul paused and took a drink of his coffee. Then he looked at Tim. "What about you? Can please stop landing yourself in the hospital? Are you going for frequent flyer miles or what?"

Tim laughed. "I think of our local hospital as a great vacation resort. I like to think of it as my home away from home." Paul shook his head and then Tim continued, "When I had my accident, it was all too real in my head that I had lost my Mary. I was really lost. I didn't know it at the time because I was spending so much time with Tiny. Little did I know that Tiny was very tiny. In my coma, he was about seven or so and a very rambunctious young feller. I even had a dream about Dad. That was odd. Afterward, I just kind of did what I thought was right." Tim paused for a drink of his coffee. "Paul, do you think dad is in heaven?"

"I hope so. I truly hope so."

The two sat stoic for a bit pondering the concept of their dad's eternal resting place. "How is mom?" Paul inquired. "She is doing well. A bit opinionated. A bit bold. A bit motherly," Tim replied coyishly. The men giggled.

"I am glad you came, Tim. I have missed you."

"You have missed my wife, don't be toying with me."

"You caught me."

Finishing up their coffee, both men agreed that now that the gas tanks were fuel, they needed their energy fueled as well. They agreed to go to the diner and grab a bite to eat.

When the two entered the diner, Kim was behind the counter. She could hardly recognize them without their brotherly love costumes on and their antics prevailing. The men took a seat at the counter and ordered. Between customers, Kim would make small talk. They fought over who was going to pay and leave a tip, when Kim explained that the bill was on her today. And not to argue with a tired waitress. They both replied, "Yes, ma'am."

Tim looked at Paul in the parking lot and asked if he wanted to go to annoy Mary. They would do a search and destroy her peace mission. Paul laughed and said that he would rather just go for a walk and talk to his brother; it had been too long. Tim agreed.

Paul took Tim to the shop. He showed him his little sanctuary. Paul explained how it came to be, and how it was what has helped him stay grounded. The two compared stories and giggled that they each had the same pastor…by name anyway. Paul went into detail about Kim and Alex and inquired to Tim about his thoughts. The two spoke of the coincidence of where the shop was located in how Paul was placed in the line of travel for this family. They discussed Paul's trip back to God and how he was able to help Kim and Alex find their way. Tim explained that this was not random by any means. This was all planned. Paul stated that now, he sees it. However, why him? Tim giggled and said, "That is one I cannot answer because I am struggling with that very question."

The men went over to park and walked around, as Tim regaled the tale of Colton and how he came into their lives. Paul listened intently. Paul asked Tim if he by chance had a picture of Colton. Tim produced his phone and stated that if he could figure the blasted thing out…maybe. Paul giggled and took the phone away from Tim. Tim snatched it back and said, "Give me a chance." They laughed and Tim pulled up his pictures. The first several were of him and Tiny playing or hanging out watching television and eating whatever. Tim finally found a picture of him and Colton after Colton dedicated his life to Christ. Paul studied the picture and said, "He looks like Alex." Tim took the phone and looked very closely to the picture. Paul pulled up a picture he had of Alex, and they compared. They were twins.

Astonished and bewildered, the two men agreed to pass this by Mary before approaching Kim and definitely not Alex. Tim looked at Paul and asked, "Who was that battle buddy that you thought Alex looked like? I am very curious now. Colton served and has many battle scars." Paul looked at the picture again and said, "My friend was James. But I learned about a month ago, that he had lost his life on the last deployment to a roadside bomb."

Tim and Paul headed back to Paul's. Tim called Mary and asked her to join them. He explained that they needed her expert advice. Though he said it jokingly, Mary could tell by his tone that he was only playing slightly.

Chapter Seven

Mary arrived at Paul's. They described their dilemma and then showed her the photos. Mary studied the photos. Each detail of them. Comparing, scrutinizing, and wondering. Could Alex be Colton's? In all their talks, he never mentioned or even hinted that he may be a father. Each time they spoke of secrets, she always assumed that it had to do with things he had to do on deployment to survive. As they talked about what they did know, what they did see—all three of them—the coincidence of it all…they all agreed that they needed to consult an outside party who would be impartial. They decided to seek out Tom's counsel.

Paul called Tom and asked him if they could meet at the church. Tom obliged graciously. Because of the tendency for Paul to be seen more often now at his home or business, he did not want to draw attention and get any surprising guests before they got some guidance.

Tom met them at the church office. He offered coffee or water and then got himself a cup. "So now that all the awkward pleasantries are out of the way, what's up?"

"Tom, I want you to look at these pictures and tell me what you think?" Paul replied. Then both Paul and Tim handed their phones over to Tom. Cautiously, Tom took them. He smiled at the picture of Alex, then shock covered his face.

Mary inquired, "Based on your facial expression, you see the same thing we do?"

Tom sat his coffee down after another sip and studied the pictures closely without saying a word. After a few minutes, he asked, "Has anyone talked to Kim?"

All three shook their heads, and Paul said, "We wanted your counsel before we did anything. We think we know what to do, but if we all see the same thing, it is life-changing…for everyone."

Entertaining another drink of coffee and the uncanny resemblance in the pictures. Tom asked, "Tim, Mary, how long are you here for?"

Mary replied, "Our flight leaves tomorrow at four in the afternoon."

Stroking his chin, Tom sat pondering how to approach the elephant in the room with the least amount of disturbance in the force of nature. "I believe that we need to approach Kim first. No need to notify Alex until we know if there is a need to notify him. I do not want to stir any unnecessary emotions. We need facts and the only one here that has them is Kim. Paul, do you know what time she gets off work?"

Paul answered that it should be any time now; her normal shift ends at two thirty, and as long as she is not working over, then anytime. Tom decided that he would call her and ask her to come to the church for a minute. That would not be as odd as if Paul were to ask. Tom had often asked for Kim's help in delicate matters around the church so this would be normal.

When Kim arrived, she noticed Paul's car and the rental she had seen Tim driving. Confused, she entered the office to find all of them sitting there. All the men stood as she came in. "Um, what is going on? Is Alex okay?" Kim's voice trembled a bit. Tom explained that Alex was fine, but they were at a place in a problem where they needed her help. Still confused, she agreed, and Tom handed her Tim's phone with a picture of Colton pulled up. Kim dropped the phone then covered her face. Tim picked up his phone. Mary got up and put her arm around Kim. "I got a letter from a guy named James that said he was Cole's friend and that Cole had been killed by a roadside bomb. When I received that, I decided that I would just keep it all to myself. I did not want to burden Alex with…" Kim started to cry as Mary held her close.

The men stood in silence. Mary held her close and told her it was okay. A few minutes passed. Kim got herself together and looked at them to ask, "Where is he?"

Mary looked at her and explained that Colton was living with her and Tim. That he had come to them last year when he was in a very low and dark place. That he has many demons that he has not spoken of, and they had no idea he was a father. Mary explained that if Kim wanted, they would assist in reuniting. Kim told them that she needed to go home and process all this. She also had to figure out how to tell Alex. She needed time. All agreed to keep their place and wait for her lead.

Chapter Eight

Kim was sitting in the front room staring out the window when Alex came bolstering in. "Hey, Mom, I am home." Kim did not answer. She was deep in thought. How was she going to explain this to him? How was he going to receive it? How could Colton hide from her like this? So many emotions. So many thoughts. So many…

"Hey! What…you don't even acknowledge your favorite son?" Alex said with a chuckle as he plopped down on the couch. "Mom… you here, it's me Alex…your son."

Kim looked up and smiled. "Yes, of course, you are my favorite son. I was just thinking."

Alex interrupted, "Ya think? I haven't seen you that deep in thought for a long time." With a devilish smile, he added, "You thinking about that hot rod you gonna buy me, Mommy?"

Kim, with her best sarcastic tone, replied, "You bet, stud."

After Alex finished his snack, he said, "Okay. Seriously. What's up? You have this really weird look on your face."

"I…" Kim paused and took a deep breath. "I have something I need to talk to you about. I am not sure how to even start." Kim turned her gaze to Alex, who by now was completely attuned to his mother's voice. The last time heard this tone was when she told him his grandpa died.

Before she could continue, he blurted, "Is Paul okay?" his voice shaking.

Confused, Kim calmed him and affirmed that Paul was just fine. "Alex," she began, "the news I have for you is still new to me, so I am not sure how to explain it. So I am going to ask you to please not interrupt me, no matter what questions pop into your mind. Let me tell you this story, and at the very end, I will answer all your questions. I promise. Do I have your word as a man?" Kim paused.

Alex looked at the odd demeanor of his mother's composure and agreed to her terms. He truly had no idea what she was talking about.

Kim proceeded to recall her youth and how Alex came to be. She had met Cole at a gathering she had attended many years ago. They had become quite a couple. He had been stationed near where she had lived, and this particular party was for a mutual friend, Dave. Dave was getting married, and this was the announcement party. Cole and I met at the snack bar where we both were trying to hide. Though they were happy for Dave, there were just too many people. They kind of bumped into each other going after a slider. She continued to explain how they became close friends, and she had been there each time he deployed and when he returned. They did not see each other as a "couple" but not just friends either. It was a solid friendship. She assured Alex that she was no "ho" and that sex was never part of their relationship…until Cole returned from the last deployment. He came back seeking a commitment. They had been the "uncouple" faithfully for three years and two-year-long deployments.

Kim paused for a minute then continued. "I agreed, and we became a couple-couple. Cole was the light of my day and the stars of my night. One night, we were out to dinner, and he proposed. He did the whole ordeal. Down on one knee, fancy dinner, music… everything. It was beautiful. I accepted with a flood of tears running down my face. My Prince Charming had arrived.

"We had planned to be married the next month, trying to give those we really wanted time to make arrangements to come if they could. It was going to be a small engagement, just those who we were close to. Then, the week before we had planned, his unit was put on alert and deployed within seventy-two hours. As soon as he hit the base, he was locked down, and there was nothing we could do. Twenty-four hours later, he flew. Two months later, I got a letter from a guy named James stating that Cole had been killed in a roadside bombing. I was devastated. I had gotten sick and could not even make myself get out of bed. Finally, a friend got me to go see a doctor, and I found out I was pregnant with you."

She took a breath and looked at her son's face. The first time since she had started recalling the tale. Tears were in his eyes. He was meeting his father for the first time. Still confused as to why she had never told him before but intent on listening and learning. Question upon question upon question was building in his head, but he had given his word and sat respectfully.

Kim continued, "After the letter, then finding out I was carrying his child, I had to decide if I should give you his last name or not. I chose not, so as not to have to always be bombarded with questions about our different last names. It was just easier for me to give you my name. You never really asked me about your dad, so I never had to tell you anything. Once in a while, you would comment about not having a dad, and I wanted to tell you that he was a hero, but I always chickened out."

"Mom, I know I promised to wait, but…why are you telling me now?"

"Alex, your father is alive."

Alex fell silent. His face went stoic and confused. Mountains of questions penetrated his mind. Throughout the maze of his own questions, he could hear a whisper of dissident chaos trying to make its way to the forefront. (*He knew about you and chose not to be a part of your life. He does not love you. He was no hero. He is a coward.*)

"How do you know he is alive?" Alex inquired.

"Today, Pastor Tom asked me to come to the church to help him with a delicate matter. When I got there, Paul, Tim, and Mary were there. Tim had a picture of your dad on his phone. Your dad is alive."

Chapter Nine

Kim and Alex talked into the night about Cole. Kim told stories of how playful and spontaneous he was. She regaled of tales of late-night movies and pizza. Nights where he spent the night on the couch. As she told each story, a light of life would glimmer in her eyes. Alex listened and watched her reactions to each tale. He was enthralled by her recollection and memories of the man who stole her heart. He had never seen this much happiness in her face. She was beaming.

When Kim had told her last gut-busting story, Alex asked, "Mom, I have a question. Why didn't he want us? Why did he pretend to be dead?"

Kim replied, "I don't know, Alex. I don't know. What I do know is that something very terrible must have happened for him to ghost me like that. He was always very protective of me. Maybe he thought I needed protecting. What I do know is that I am hungry and need a sandwich, would you like one too?"

"Yes, ma'am," Alex answered. Kim leaned over and gave her son a peck on the forehead. She had not done that since he was about fourteen when he expressed that he was too old for such things.

Alex sat on the sofa and watched as his mom danced into the kitchen to make sandwiches. She was happy. But why did this guy want to be dead to her if he loved her so much.

He ghosted your mom. He never really loved her. He just wanted "a companion." An evil-type eerie voice whispered throughout Alex's mind. He had thought after thought after thought about what a jerk this guy was, but he was having difficulty being mad because his mom was happy.

Across town, Tim and Mary began packing. They had been silent pretty much since Kim left the church office. *Knock, knock.* The two looked at each other in disbelief and then Tim answered the door. "Paul?"

"Hey, guys. I can't think. I am worried about Kim and Alex. I kind of thought I would hear something from Alex, but not one sound. Do you think I should go check on them?" Distress was all over Paul's face.

Mary put down the clothes she was folding for the suitcase and went over to hug Paul. "Paul, we cannot do anything right now but wait. They need time to process the news and then decide to act on it or not act on it," Mary explained.

"Paul, I understand how you feel," Tim started. "I want so much to call Colton and let him know he has a son, but I can't. I have to wait on Kim and Alex."

The three sat down and Mary made a pot of coffee for them. "Tom said it best after Kim left his office, we must pray about this. We must pray a covering over everyone. This is life-changing. We do not know why he disappeared from Kim's life. Why he didn't want to be a father. Why he would lie about being dead. We have no answers to very probing questions. We need to pray for guidance and under-standing," Tim stated as he sat down. "I know that I am fighting off very angry feelings toward Colton. I feel like I have been lied to and taken advantage of, but then I wonder what happened that would have caused him to do this and find mercy. This God thing is very confusing sometimes. And don't get me started on that stupid little voice who is telling me call and kick him out before he robs us blind."

Tim was getting riled up when there came another knock at the door. Mary was already up, so she answered it. "Pastor Tom?"

"Good evening, everyone. How are you doing? I am a bit of a mess myself, thank you for not jumping on the 'fine' train," he said with a smirky smile. The three gave off a half-hearted chuckle; Mary poured four cups of coffee and sat down. "Pastor, we were just getting ready to pray. We are all hearing the voices of dismay and dissent. Telling us to judge harshly. Then telling us that Kim is to blame. There is too much unknown, and we really need that covering you spoke of earlier."

Tom took a sip of his coffee then chuckled that it was hot. Mary agreed that it was hot and that she would work on making not hot but hot coffee. The group sat their cups on the table, joined hands, bowed their heads, and began to pray one by one, then in unison, then one by one again. Each person casting out and binding or asking for guidance. All reciting that "where two or more are gathered, you are there. We are standing on that promise."

As they closed the prayer, they were still holding hands when Tim asked, "Did you hear that?"

The others looked at him oddly. They sat in silence. Still holding hands. Then Paul asked, "Did you hear that?"

Tim asked if he was mocking him, Paul assured him that he was not. While the two of them created a stare down, Mary and Tom recited in unison, "Be still."

Paul and Tim looked at them and then back at each other. Then they repeated, "And know that I am God."

Tim asked if it was cold in the room and reached for his coffee. Paul agreed. The four of them sat and talked for about an hour on the subject of what had just happened. Tom stated that he had never experienced anything like that before and that the hair on the back of his neck stood up. Tim explained that he has had similar experiences, but he always seems to be unconscious when they happened. He looked at Paul and said, "Pinch me."

Paul pulled back and slugged him in the arm. Tim hollered and said, "I said 'pinch' not punch." Paul stated that he was just making sure. Mary shook her head and retreated into her thoughts. She had known Colton for many years yet never knew he a serious lady friend. What was going on here.

As the night grew later, Tom and Paul bid their adieu and left. Mary finished working on the suitcase while Tim changed into his pajamas and began to ask her questions. Mary explained that she was just as lost as he was, but until they spoke to Kim and Alex, they would have no answers. Mary did pose a question back, however. "Tim, what would you think about extending our stay here for a couple more days?"

Tim looked at his beautiful wife and said, "You took the words right out of my mouth. We have flexible tickets. I will make the arrangements first thing in the morning."

Chapter Ten

"Hey, Lucas, can you come over? I need to talk to someone. Tim and Mary are not home yet. They extended their stay, I guess. I could really use a friend," Colton asked Lucas over the phone.

"Sure, give me about an hour, I am in the middle of something, and then I can bud. Or...is it an emergency?" Lucas replied.

"No, it is not an emergency. I just have some things I need to talk out and was hoping you could help me figure stuff."

"Not a problem. Like I said, give me about an hour, and I will be over. You didn't burn the house down, did you?" Lucas said with a chuckle.

Giggling, he answered, "Not yet. See you in an hour. If I am not at the house, I will be at the creek. I am going to go sit at the bridge and think."

"Got it. See you in a bit."

Colton hung up the phone, grabbed a bottle of water, and headed for the creek. Traipsing down the path, the ugly voice began whispering, but he was able to brush it off. There was something about this place where the voices did not bother him as much. He could shut them out. This was the most peace he had felt in such a long time. He did not want this feeling to end.

Colton made his way to the bridge and found a suitable spot to pop a squat. The day was perfect for enjoying nature. Sitting with his feet over the edge of the bridge, the soles of his boots barely skimming the creek, Colton became mesmerized by the sweet smell and gentle breeze coming off the brook. He was at peace. His mind began to wander, almost to the point of hypnosis. He was completely trans-fixed on his surroundings.

You cannot hide here from me. I can get you no matter where you go. You cannot hide from your past. You cannot hide from your past. You cannot hide from your past.

"Hey, dude," Lucas said, "what's with the face?"

Colton jolted, "Whaaat?"

With a slight chuckle, he pointed out, "You okay? You had this weird look on your face."

"Sorry, have a seat. I really need to talk to someone. I normally talk to Mary or Tim, but like I told you on the phone, they have been delayed. I thought about Pastor Tom, but he has heard so much of my problems, I think he needs a break from me." He paused with a slight smirk.

"What's going on? I will help if I can." Lucas could feel the change in Colton and was worried about his friend.

"First, thank you for coming over. I need to remember my manners. I don't need my mom or Mary to knock me out over that." Both men laughed.

"No problem, my friend. So spill it. What is bugging you?" Lucas inquired.

"Okay. I need you to hear me out. Just listen. I have never told anyone this. No one. Not even Mary. No one knows. I need to know that you won't spill it all over town. Promise me." Colton looked at Lucas with pleading eyes. "I have to tell someone, and I trust you as much as I trust Tim and Mary, please give me your word."

"You have my word…I promise," Lucas agreed.

Colton began to tell a story of long ago. A story of when he was in the military. When he had some of the best pals a guy could have. They had each other's back no matter what. If one messed up, they all took the fall. There were times when they all were on extra duty because one of them did something stupid, but the others would not give him up. They had a bond like no other. They were considered musketeers, though there were four of them all together. Colton told stories of practical jokes, broken hearts, fear of dying, survival of another attack, rescues of the oppressed, long nights of drinking, and even a few nights of prayer. He told of times when they all had to wash the trucks because of their pranks. He told of times when they hid all the utensils for the field mess, and they were forced to use their bayonets. He told of times when they were not sure they would make it out of a situation only to prevail. They believed that they were unstoppable as long as they each had their backs. Colton paused.

Looking down at the water, he said, "Their names were… Michael…James…and…Scott." He continued, "On November 11, Veterans' Day no less. On November 11, I got detailed to help in command. They all called me a suck-up. I just told them I was that good. They were tasked to piggyback with another squad to go on patrol. They never made it back. They were killed by a roadside bomb. I lost my pack on that November 11 day." Tears were flowing fiercely down Colton's face. Catching his breath, he continued, "I should have been with them. I should have been in that truck. I should have died. Lucas, why didn't I die?"

In complete shock at what he just heard, Lucas was speechless. His pal was pleading, and he did not know how to answer him. "Colton…I don't know. But I can tell you this, I am glad you did not die that day. You are important to me. To Tim. To Mary."

Colton wiped some of the tears from his face then continued, "I went on every and I mean every mission after that. I did everything I could. I put myself in harm's way as much as I could. I did everything I could do to get killed, but I lived. I don't know why. I should have died with them. I should have been in the truck with them. But… that is not the worst of it."

Lucas, trying his best to be a good friend but realizing that this is way out of his whimsical wheelhouse, wrapped his arm around Colton's shoulders and pulled him next to him. "What could be worse? Did you kill someone that you were not supposed to?" Lucas said without knowing what else to say.

Taking a deep breath to compose himself, Colton said, "Before I deployed the last time, I proposed to the most beautiful gal on this planet. She said yes. Somewhere around a week before we were going to be married, I was deployed. After all this with my musketeers went down, I was not right. I have demons, even today, in my head. I am not the man she fell in love with, and I did not want to be one of those come home wrong and ruin everything kind of stories. So I pretended to be James and wrote her a letter telling her that I had died. I knew that because we were not married, and we had not done any of the paperwork, she would not be notified by anyone other than a battle buddy and I was sure that I could pull it off. But…the demons have eaten me alive. Until I came home, and Mary took me in…I was one of those statistics. Lucas, I need help. I cannot do this alone anymore."

In silence, Lucas held his friend. He had no words. He had no wisdom. He only wanted to help. After Colton had completed his tale of anguish, Lucas asked, "Have you ever tried to contact your fiancé since you wrote the letter? Or just try and find her to see if you could find her?"

Still sobbing, Colton explained that he could not do that to her. He had made his bed, and he was forced to live out his life with regret of his decision.

Lucas continued to sit with Colton all afternoon. They sat at the brook feeling the gentle breeze blow. Every now and then, Colton would recall another antic of him and his musketeers. Lucas would laugh and listen. Colton unleashed all of his past, his journeys, his problems, the voices that he hears. He explained that the voices are not as bad here…on Mary's property. That he was not sure why, but he feels safe here.

As the sun began to set, the temperature began to fall as well. Neither gent was wearing a jacket, so they made their way up to the house. They sat down at the table and drank a cup of coffee. They watched the sun close on the day. Lucas sat with his friend well into the night. They talked about this, that, and the other thing. Lucas tried to help his friend with little spirits of his characters, such as the monarch or dragon slayer. He had no idea how to comfort his friend. He had no idea what he was supposed to do to help him find peace. Was he supposed to guide him somewhere…if so, where. Lucas was at a loss. In light of not having a direction, he did what he did best, he was a whimsical friend, full of optimism.

"Colton, can I ask you a question?" Lucas inquired.

"Sure. What could I possible tell you now that I have spilled my guts to you.?" he said with a smirk of relief.

"What is your fiancé's name?"

"Why do you want to know that?"

"Well, since you don't want to be a burden to her, I thought maybe I could have a crack at her," he said with a cheesy smile.

Colton smiled and giggled. "Dude, she would chew you up and spit you out. She is a feisty one."

"So you are saying you are going to try again, and I need to follow the 'bro code'?"

Looking down at his empty coffee cup, Colton whispered, "Kim. Her name is Kim."

"Thanks, pal. I am sure I am the right man for her. Now all I have to do is find *Kim*. That should be easy enough…that is not a popular name."

Both men began to laugh, but Lucas could see the devastating pain in Colton's eyes. He wanted so hard to help his friend. But he sincerely had no idea how. Colton thanked Lucas for listening and trying to make him feel better. They polished off the last of the coffee, and Lucas left. He had offered to stay, but Colton said that he was exhausted and just wanted some sleep. Lucas promised to check on him in the morning, and they said their good nights.

Chapter Eleven

"God, I need your help. My friend is hurting. He has a lot of things going on. He only feels sanctuary at Tim and Mary's. His mind is in turmoil. He has done things that he is not proud of. He has lost a part of himself. He does not know what to do. He opened up to me God. To me. Why me? Why did you pick me? It does not make any sense. I am not a counselor. I am not a pastor or minister. I am not a therapist. He needed someone that knew what to do. I have no idea." Lucas pleaded with God to help him help his friend.

Before he could finish his prayer, he heard a still, small voice. "Do you believe?"

Lucas was taken back, and again, he heard a still, small voice, "Do you believe, Lucas?"

"*God.* Are you talking to me God? Really talking to me?"

"Lucas, answer me. Do you believe in me and my power?"

Lucas pulled his car over to the park parking lot and shut it off. The sun was down, and the lights were coming on. "God, I am here. I do believe. I do believe. Why did you choose me, Lord? I am a nobody. Why did you choose me?"

"Lucas, I am the I AM. I am the Lord Almighty. You are my chosen. The name that you seek is Harrison."

"GOD! GOD! WHAT DOES THAT MEAN?"

Lucas sat in his car, screaming and praying for God to speak to him again. He was not sure what was going on. It felt cool that he spoke to him, but then he felt like he was just losing his mind. A chill entered his car and inaudible sounds came from the back seat; he turned around, but no one was there. He began to get scared, then like magic, the fear was gone. He was still confused. He still did not understand what was happening. He still had no clue what he was doing or what God meant. What was the name Harrison that God said he was looking for. Who was Harrison?

Lucas sat in his car for nearly an hour talking to God, trying to figure out what he was telling him. He prayed for guidance and understanding and sat quietly hoping to hear that still small voice again. Processing everything that had happened today with Colton, then this encounter with God, Lucas was overwhelmed. Staring into the night sky over the park, he sought glimmers of something. Anything that would bring understanding. He noticed on the far side of the playground, a set of intense eyes in the trees. As he focused in on those eyes, another pair appeared. Both sets seemed to be trans-fixed on him…at least it seemed that way to him. He could not divert from this new audience.

Tap, tap, tap.

Lucas jolted a little and looked out the driver's window. His eyes were met with a blinding light from a flashlight. He rolled down his window and said, "Yes, sir."

The officer asked, "Sir, are you all right? We had a report of a suspicious vehicle in the park."

Lucas got turned around in his seat and said, "Max?"

The officer replied, "Lucas? What are you doing here? Ain't it past your bedtime."

With a slight chuckle, Lucas replied, "I was just thinking about something and praying. I pulled off here so that I would not pull off into a ditch for not paying attention."

Max replied, "Are you okay? Anything I can help you with?"

Lucas answered, "No, Max. This is one I have to figure out on my own. Thanks. I will head for the house now. My owl friends seem to have left their perch over there. They were keeping me company."

The two chuckled and traded some friendly barbs. Max called in all clear to his dispatch and left. Lucas looked around for the owls, but they seemed to have lost interest in him. When he got home and ready for bed, it was nearly midnight. It was past his bedtime. *I won-der how long I was at the park*, he thought. With his nightly routine behind him, Lucas sat on the edge of his bed and began to pray. He thanked God for this day and all the blessings. He praised God for his mercies. He thanked him for having so much faith in him to help Colton. He did ask again why him but followed with "You have your reasons. I will do my best." He closed out his prayer asking God to cover Colton and protect him from his demons and to enlighten him on the path he needed to travel to help his friend. After his prayer, Lucas curled up in his bed and fell fast asleep.

"Colton, stop. Don't do it. Let's talk it out." Lucas was in a panic. What could he do? Colton was on the edge of a precipice and in the motion of jumping. What was he going to do to stop him? Colton had already warned that he was going to jump. He could not handle the demons anymore. Everyone would be better off without him. "What about Tim and Mary? How do you think they will feel? They opened their home to you and trusted you. They have taken you in, and…this will devastate them," Lucas pleaded with Colton. "Colton…I know her name is Kim Harrison."

Just as he was about to fall forward, he felt a tug backward. Lucas was able to sneak up on him and grab his shirt, preventing him from falling. "Her name is Kim Harrison."

Ring, ring, ring, ring.

Lucas jumped up out of bed. Looking around, he saw that it was just his alarm clock going off. Wiping the sleep from his eyes and stretching, he sat on the edge of his bed and wondered if he really had even been asleep. What a dream. More like a nightmare. Lucas began his morning routine. While he was brushing his teeth, the name *Kim Harrison* came to mind. Thinking out loud with a mouth full of toothpaste, "Who is Kim Harrison?" Lucas finished preparing for the day and headed off for the diner. He had promised Ayla that he would meet her for breakfast.

"Hello, my sweet love," Lucas greeted Ayla.

"Hello, my prince charming," she replied.

The two found a seat and began to converse about different things around the area. Ayla asked how Lucas was doing because he seemed a little more off than usual. With quick wit, he let her know that he was just as weird today as he was yesterday. As the two completed their meal, Lucas told Ayla that he needed to talk to her after she got off work. He explained that it would be a talk of hypotheticals, but not really hypothetical. With a bewildered look, she agreed to meet with him later in the day after her shift.

Lucas left the diner and headed out to Tim and Mary's to talk to Colton. He had to talk to him about his dream. When he pulled into the drive, he realized that he was about to break a promise and quickly texted Ayla to say that he had to retract the meeting because of a promise. Ayla let him know that it was all right, but if he needed to talk, she was there for him.

Lucas knocked on the door, but there was no answer. That meant either Colton was sleeping in, or he was out back somewhere. He made his way behind the house and stopped by the shop. He could see that no one had been in there for what appeared to be a couple of days, so he headed to the brook. On his walk back, he heard "Her name is Kim Harrison" in his mind. He stopped and whispered, "God, is that you?" Standing silent for a few moments, he did not hear anything else, but that was now the second time that he had heard that name but had no reference to what it meant. Lucas made his way to the brook, but there was no Colton. He presumed that Colton must be sleeping in, so he took a moment to have a seat on the bridge. This area was quite tranquil, and though he did not get to come back here often, he did not want to miss an opportunity for glorious peace.

Sitting on the bridge, he began to remember the dream he had had. Why would he have such a thought about Colton committing suicide. He had battled these demons this long; what would put him over the edge like that? Add to that this name. Kim Harrison. Lucas watched as the chipmunks and squirrels scurried about playfully but purposefully. He witnessed a couple of robins dancing in the sky. The brook was moving but not as fast as you would have thought after the couple of good rains they had received.

"God, I know you are talking to me. I know you are giving me clues. But I don't understand. Who is Kim Harrison?"

"She is the girl I told you about last night. How did you find her last name?" Colton said as he came up from behind.

Lucas jumped up and explained that the name came to him in a dream. He explained that he had no idea that the name was the full identity of whom Colton was talking about. After a few minutes of expository debate, Colton took a seat on the bridge and Lucas sat down beside him.

"'Colton, I want to help you. How can I help you?" Lucas inquired. "God had you call me for a reason, and I am not sure why, but he did. How can I help you?"

Colton sat stoic, watching the squirrels and the chipmunks. "I just needed a friend last night, Lucas. I had to get that off my chest. I have not been able to let anyone in, not even Mary. What kind of monster am I that I turned my back on the one woman who loved me for who I am. But I am not that person anymore. I want to find her, but I am sure that she has made a life for herself, it has been seventeen years since I sent that letter. I am all alone."

The two sat on the bridge, Colton told of more antics from his musketeer days. Lucas implanted himself into the stories and made-up new adventures. The two men laughed at the entire concocted nonsense. Lucas reassured Colton that no one knew his secrets but told him about the dream he had last night. Colton looked back at Lucas with astonishment and explained that he had the same dream. Not really understanding the significance, the two decided to pray together for guidance and a covering from the enemy. Lucas made his way back to his car and then went directly home.

On his way home, Lucas got the idea of checking out social media for Kim Harrison. What would it hurt? He tried several variations of spelling and got so many hits that he was convinced that he would never be able to single one out of this massive bunch. He walked away and completed some other tasks. He had forgotten about the search and went to bed after a long day of chores.

His alarm went off in the morning as usual, and he started his morning routine. He had almost forgotten entirely the search when out of the corner of his eye, a glimmer caught his attention. As he turned to see what it was, his gaze crossed the hallway, and he could see his computer was lit up. Still not thinking about the search, Lucas went in to shut down the laptop when he noticed a news article about a guy named Paul getting an award. There was a picture of this man and a young man beside him that looked remarkably like Colton.

Taken aback by the remarkable resemblances. Lucas began to read the story around these two men. As he entered into the realm of the story, he recognized the last name of the man being honored, and it was Tim's last name. Staring at the content of the story, Lucas recalled that Tim and Mary were going to visit Tim's brother. *Could this be true?* Lucas's mind took off in a flat-out race to find out if he had found someone Colton could speak to and possibly find this Kim lady.

Chapter Twelve

"Mary, are you about ready? We need to head to the airport soon," Tim inquired.

"Yes, dear. I am. Just praying some more for clarity and a blessing for Kim and Alex. This is going to be an adjustment for sure," Mary responded.

"Did you get with Mom and have her start preparing a place for them to stay? Was she okay with this?" Tim asked.

"Martha was just fine. She said that big ole house of hers needed some fresh air running through it. She promised not to say anything. She was just going to tell the kids that Uncle Paul was coming for a visit. That we should be pulling in about five," Mary responded.

"Mom, are you okay?" Alex asked his mother.

"Yeah, I think so. I have a lot of weird thoughts running through my mind. Like little whispers that I am wasting my time. Never had that before." She paused. "I am nervous. I have not seen him since before you were born. But I am excited as well." Then she asked, "Are you ready?"

Alex looked at his mom and said, "I want to stay home."

Perplexed, Kim looked at Alex and asked why. He answered, "I think you need to take the lead on this. You need to see what happened. I think my presence would confuse things. I am not ready to be rejected by my father." Kim put down her bag and pulled Alex close to her. Holding him as tightly as she could, she told him that she understood but wished he would change his mind. She would really like his moral support. Even if he did not meet Cole, she would like him to be there so that she had a familiar face. After the embrace,

Alex said that he would go. He just wanted to make sure that Kim wanted him to go for him not obligation. Kim slugged his arm and told him to get in the car. Alex smiled and said, "Yes, ma'am…you hit like a girl."

Tim and Mary swung by and picked up Paul. His bag was packed, and he was ready sitting on the front porch. As he was loading his bag into the trunk, a car pulled up in front of the drive blocking them in. It was Melony. "Paul, I understand that you are going home for a while. Will you do me a favor? Will you give this to your mother for me. It is a picture of all of us…with Carter. I don't think I ever sent her one."

Paul graciously took the picture and told her that he would gladly give the photo to his mom. Tim, Mary, and Paul loaded up into the car. Melony left with peace in her heart. The three headed for and met Kim and Alex there. Mary could tell that Kim was anxious and that Alex was playing the strong silent type. Tim looked at Alex and asked him if he had ever been in airplane before, with a nervous chuckle Alex explained that he had not and that it was bit nerve-racking. He knew that they were mostly safe, but the unknown was always and has always been a thing with him. Tim assured him that he checked with the airline, and they had very experienced pilot today. He has had his license from Pilots 1012 discount for six whole months. Mary reached out and pushed Tim's shoulder telling him to behave.

They must have had a good tail wind because the flight seemed shorter. Tim did not get as good a nap as he did on his flight out to Paul's. Jon had agreed to meet them at the airport since he had a big-enough vehicle to transport them all and their luggage. Jon and Paul kicked up a conversation and talked the entire trip home. As they pulled into Martha's drive, she stood on the porch in anxious anticipation. She had not seen Paul in several years nor had they spoken. It had been difficult. As they pulled into the drive, Jon told his uncle Paul that he had to report to Grandma, or he would be taken to the woodshed. Paul acknowledged the requirement and did not hesitate. Jon explained that he would get the bags. Martha and Paul embraced and held on to each other for an eternity. Paul attempted to whisper in her ear, but she hushed him and allowed his love to embody her soul.

Kim and Alex thanked Martha for allowing them to stay with her. She let them know that it was no big deal and that she had plenty of room for everyone.

Once everyone was comfy in their rooms, they gathered at the dining room table for a spot of tea. Tim, trying to be funny, asked his mother for a shot of whiskey, which got him a stern eye and a huge laugh from Alex. Martha swiftly turned to Alex and said, "Young man," to which Alex stopped in his tracks. Then all at once everyone started laughing.

Paul explained the entire ordeal to his mother. Martha asked Kim how she was feeling, and without any hesitation, she replied that she did not know. "To be honest, I have no feelings but tons of them all at the same time."

"Dear, I would assume so. Tomorrow morning, I will make us a good breakfast. Tim, I want you to be here about 10:00 a.m. You can pick up Kim and take her to your house. I think the original encounter should be just the two of you. Alex, if you would be so kind, you can stay here and help me make some desserts. Have you ever baked before?" With a confused look on his face, he said that he had not, but that he had tried to set their apartment on fire a few times. Martha explained that there would be no fires but lots of taste testing and sampling required of him. Alex was game.

Chapter Thirteen

Tim and Paul went for a quick stroll around the yard to talk. "How are you doing, Paul?" Tim inquired. "You are putting up a good front, but how are you doing? It's me. Let me in."

Paul rubbed his chin and looked at his brother. He began to speak when Tim warned him about trying to be the strong, silent type. Paul smiled and said, "I am fighting a bunch of emotions right now. I want to sympathize with this man and try to understand where he is coming from, but..." He paused. "But I also want to go over to your place and beat the tar out of him for doing this. I know he did not know about Alex, but you have a son. I...I have become very protective of Alex. I do not want him to get hurt in this situation. He is innocent of all this. I also don't want Alex to try and be the 'man' and protect his mom, thus causing a bigger issue. I want to make this right, but I want this to be right. It is a lot...I just hope that I can keep it together tomorrow morning."

With a bit of a smirky smile, Tim replied to Paul's plea, "If you want, we can trade places." Paul was confused. Tim continued, "You can go to my place, not say a word about what you know, and try to only focus on antics that were pulled while you were away from home then come over here in the morning, again without saying a word, take Kim back to the house, and pray that lightning does not strike the house when they both set eyes on each other."

Paul looked at Tim, took a deep breath, and said, "Good luck with that. I will just sit here and sulk." They both smiled and gave each other a bear hug. They continued to walk and talk. It was getting late when Tim heard the familiar voice: "Boys." Tim and Paul both stopped in their tracks and recited, "Yes, ma'am."

"Time to come in. We all have a big day tomorrow." Martha had asserted her presence outside and the two of them snapped too as if they were ten again.

As Tim and Paul made their way around the house, Alex came out to see the commotion. He thought it was quite entertaining to watch two grown men tuck tail like that and so quickly. Proudly displaying a "Haha! You got in trouble" look on his face, Alex smarted off, "Boyssss." Alex did not realize that Martha was still in the doorway. She cleared her throat, "Young man."

Alex snapped around and whispered, "Yes, ma'am." Tim and Paul lost all composure and began laughing hysterically at Alex and the look on his face. Martha began to laugh as well, which set Alex's mind at ease. With all the laughter going on, Kim and Mary joined the fun on the front porch. When Tim explained what had happened, Kim looked at Martha and asked her to come home with them, she could use some back up with Alex. That sent everyone into another fit of laughter.

"Hey, everyone, what is so funny. Can we join you?"

Tim looked up to see Lucas and Colton standing on the sidewalk, smiling, wanting to join in the fun. Tim then nudged Paul who looked up, and the two of them became instantly silent. Martha turned to see who had joined them in the yard and said, "Lucas. Colton. What a surprise." At the sound of Colton's name, Alex became stoic…unsure of what to do next. Mary came over to Paul and Tim. Kim stepped out from behind Martha and slowly made her way down the steps. As she made her way to the yard, Colton's huge playful grin faded into astonished fear. Lucas did not understand what was going on until he heard Colton say, in almost a begging tone, "Kim, I am sorry." Instantly, Lucas became a statue in an awkward silence.

Nervously, Kim made her way past everyone and straight up to Colton. She raised her hands to his face and ran them slowly down, feeling each and every wrinkle, every divot, every scar, every hurt, every tear that was escaping his eyes. She placed her finger over his lips as if to signal silence. Colton stood motionless as Kim maneuvered around him, embracing his presence without embracing him. She had to be sure this was her Cole.

Everyone stood in respect for the unexpected encounter. Mary grabbed Tim's hand as tears poured out of her eyes. She watched as Kim systematically reclaimed her love for Colton. This moment was theirs. No one needed to say or do anything. Mary pulled close to Tim as she remembered her watching him in the hospital and trying to reclaim him for herself and the kids. She could see the absolute love that Kim had for him and that she was trying to reclaim it... where they left off. Mary watched as Colton stood watching his soul float around him meticulously.

The moment was surreal. The moment was magical. The moment was theirs.

Chapter Fourteen

He knew about you and did not care. He knew you were struggling and that your mom did not have anyone. He knew the trouble you were in. He saw you and did not want you. Those emotions are fake. He is not sorry. I could tell you some things. He is not a good person. He uses people. He hurts people. He purposely did not come into your life because he did not love or want you. He called your mom a whore. He let his friends know all about how he had his way then disappeared knowing that he had got her pregnant. All those stories your mom told you were lies that he led just so he could have his way with her. He set her up. He knew. He knew. He knew. He didn't care. He doesn't care. Sinister whispers penetrated Alex's mind. The darkness had been circling looking for an avenue and found Alex in dispute with his feelings and what he was witnessing. The presence took this opportunity to invade and create a caveat of doubt and anger.

Alex, with a bitter turmoil inside of showing respect for his mother's reconnection and the whispers he was hearing, quietly slid off the back of the porch and walked to the backyard. Paul saw him make a stealth exit. Paul looked up at Martha who motioned for Paul to go and check on Alex, for she, too, had seen the exit. Martha had felt a presence and had been praying for a covering; however, she was unable to command the spirit away without disturbing the moment. This would have to be dealt with differently.

Martha, indiscreetly, motioned for Tim, Mary, and Lucas to join her in the house. Carefully and silently, they each made their way to the dining room table. Martha put on a pot of coffee and tea. Mary joined her in the kitchen and asked if she could help. Martha let Mary know that there was a presence around this house that was trying to interfere and to begin praying.

"So, um, Tim…" Lucas tried to ask, "is that by chance Kim Harrison?"

Tim looked at Lucas with utter confusion. "How did you know that?"

Martha and Mary returned to the table. Lucas then proceeded to tell of Colton's confession to him a few nights earlier. He figured he could talk about with them since they knew Kim and must have an idea already since she was here. Once Lucas had finished his story, Martha expressed her concern for the presence she felt. She told them all to begin praying. She was going to call Pastor Tom and have him come join them. She felt that this situation was going to need all the warfare they could conjure. When Martha finished on the phone with Tom, she returned to the table, the group began a steadfast prayer for the presence to be dispatched and peace surround this gathering.

In the backyard, Paul caught up with Alex. He could tell that Alex was fighting a slew of emotions, sensations, and conflicts all at one time. Alex was leaning up against the tree, tears pouring from his eyes. Paul reached out, pulled him close, and held him like his own son. No words were spoken, just understanding. Alex was so filled with chaos that his body trembled. He whispered to Paul, "I am scared."

Paul latched even tighter and replied, "I am here, son. It will be all right. It will be all right."

"Paul, I can hear voices telling me that he knew all along and that he did not care about us. How could he not know about us? If he is half the man mom told me about, why didn't he come look for her…us?"

Paul held on tight and let Alex vent his concerns. He gave Alex the support he needed so that he could process what was going on. This was not the way the reuniting was supposed to happen. No one was prepared for this.

Chapter Fifteen

Colton and Kim sat on the porch steps. Still, virtually no words were spoken. Kim pulled up close to Colton. She laid her head on his chest. She could feel the pain in his skipping heart. She could sense his troubled soul. She knew he was battling demons. She knew "why" he had done what he did without him telling her. She felt it. Yes, she had questions, but she wanted to help him more than she wanted to know the answers. Her Cole had been returned to her, broken, but he had been returned.

You have screwed up. She is only waiting for the prime moment to let you have it. A whisper floated through Colton's mind. In an instant, Kim sat up. She had sensed something off. She looked at Colton and put her hands on his face, squaring her eyes to his. Tears were flowing uncontrollably from his eyes. She felt his distress and worry. Softly she caressed his cheeks and whispered, "Ignore that voice and listen to mine. I love you. I forgive you. We will work through this. Together. If you let me." He grabbed on to her for the first time in nearly twenty years and held her tightly to him. Weeping like an infant, Colton sobbed. God had brought him one step closer to peace. How was this even possible?

"Good evening. Is Martha inside?" Pastor Tom walked up the sidewalk to the porch. Paul and Alex were walking up from the back-yard when Paul explained that she was. "You must be Paul. I am Tom." Paul reached out and shook his hand.

"Well, I won't be able to forget your name." He giggled. "My pastor's name is Tom as well." The men giggled at the irony and walked up the steps past Colton and Kim to the house. Alex looked intently on his mom and this man. He could see how at peace his mom was, but his heart and mind were at war, and he just wanted justice for their hard life. Paul reached for Alex's arm to guide him inside. Alex started to say something, but Paul cleared his throat, and Alex followed him into the house.

As the three men entered the house, Martha greeted Tom. Then she introduced Paul and Alex to Lucas. She explained to Tom and Paul that there was a presence, and they had been praying. Tom let them know that as he approached the house, he could feel a fleeting attempt at deception in the air, but it was losing its ground. He did warn, though, that it was still seeking a cornerstone. Then after meeting Alex, he figured that it was Alex that he, the demon, was after because he felt peace on the front porch.

Martha asked the men if they would like a drink, and Alex asked if she had any soda. She smiled and told him that she had two different flavors in the fridge. If he liked, she would get it for him, or he was welcome to fetch it himself. He opted for himself. When he left the room, Martha asked Paul if Alex was all right. Paul stated that he is the target of the demons. He is struggling. He does not know how to feel.

The hour was getting late when Colton and Kim came into the house. "Alex," she started, "I would like you to meet your father, Cole" Alex sat at the table next to Paul. With fury in his eyes, Alex looked at and trying not to be disrespectful to his mom, he replied coldly, "This man here, Paul, is my father. I adopted him when I had no father. Nice to meet you, friend of my mother. Cole."

Silence fell over the room. It was chill. Kim tried to correct Alex, but Colton quieted her efforts. "Kim, don't."

"Mr. Harrison is a man. A man of feelings and the right to regard me as he feels appropriate. I made my choice. I have no right to insist that he feels any differently. Perhaps…perhaps one day I will earn the right to shake his hand."

Tim and Mary asked Colton if he was ready to head home. He was but he wasn't. Martha invited everyone over for morning breakfast. She explained that she was looking forward to making a huge breakfast again. It had been a long time. Kim offered to help.

Lucas politely declined, stating that he had some annoying to do in the morning with Ayla, with his youthful and playful smile. Tom expressed gratitude, but declined unless they needed him to come. He felt as though a "family" reunion would be better suited with just family. It was settled: Brunch would be served at 11:00 a.m.; come prepared to eat.

Martha hugged everyone good night. Tim, Mary, and Colton left for home. Colton sat silent in the backseat. They pulled up to the house, and Colton said that he needed to be alone. That even though it was late, he was going to the brook. He wouldn't be long, but he needed to process some things. Tim and Mary said that they understood and left him to his thoughts. Prior to them going to bed, they prayed a heavy prayer over Colton tonight as he processed the instant introduction to his unknown son. They prayed a heavy prayer for Alex. He now has a father whom he adopted and one he has never known. He is in turmoil. They prayed for Kim who seemed to be adapting, but they knew that the enemy was lurking about. Then they prayed for Paul. He has "adopted" Alex as his own; now he is competing with a ghost. Tim and Mary prayed for nearly thirty minutes, feeling that they had covered all that was needed, they climbed into bed.

"Alex," Kim whispered into his room. "Alex, are you still awake? Can we talk?"

Alex was sitting in the dark, crying silently with his thoughts. He could not process what was going on. He wanted to share in his mom's joy. He wanted to know his dad. He felt as though if he did, he would be disrespecting Paul. How could you win in this scenario. It was too much.

"Yes, Mom." He struggled. "I am awake."

"May I come in son?" she requested.

There was silence. She could hear him whimpering. Foregoing the manneristic protocols for privacy, Kim exercised her motherly rights and entered. She made her way to her son. She sat down on the floor beside him and pulled him close. She could feel his struggles as she felt Cole's. The two sat in silence for a while as she cuddled her son, just as when he was a child scared of the monsters under his bed. She brought him close so that he could hear the soothing of her heartbeat. Alex fell asleep on his mother's chest.

Paul sat up with Martha for a little longer. "Mom, I am sorry. I am sorry I have not called or written more. I love you." Paul reached over and pulled his mother close to him. Sobbing on her shoulders, with forgiveness as a plea from his own mother, Paul felt a peace he had not felt in a long time. The peace of a strong mom who loves unconditionally.

"Son, there is nothing to forgive. I love you." The two continued the embrace, then Martha stated, "But…young man," she started with a stern voice, "you ever do that again, we will make a trip to the woodshed. Understand?" She smiled, and Paul laughed.

"Yes, ma'am. I promise it won't happen again."

Chapter Sixteen

"Good morning Ms. Martha," Alex said as he entered the kitchen.

"Good morning, young man. How are you doing this morning?" Martha replied.

"May I have some orange juice please?" he asked.

"Yes, sir, you sure can. A big one or a little one?" Martha asked.

"A big one please." Alex was still wiping the sleep out of his eyes. "I am very stiff and sore this morning. I feel like I have been run over by a freight train, and they backed up to see what they hit."

With a soft smile, Martha asked, "Now I have a question. Would you allow me to give you a good-morning grandmother-type hug?"

Without hesitation, Alex grabbed her in a bear hug. "Yes, ma'am. I was hoping you were a hugger. I needed one this morning." Martha returned the loving intensity.

"Well, well, well," Paul said as he walked into the room. "Moving in on *my* mom, are ya?"

"How does a 'son' get one of those hugs?"

Without missing a beat, Alex let go of Martha and turned to Paul and gave him a bear hug too. Martha began laughing and said, "I guess just like that." With a jab to the ribs, Paul got Alex to release him. "Now, I will get my hug from *my* mom." Paul said with a sarcastic tone.

As he reached for Martha, she pulled away and asked, "Who are you again? You look familiar, but I just cannot be sure." Paul reached out to her and got his hug anyway.

Whispering in her ear, Paul asked, "You got coffee, old woman?"

Martha quickly reminded her son who was in charge with a hearty poke in the ribs and then pointed to the coffee pot.

Alex laughed at Paul as he doubled over and Paul, licking his wounds and rethinking his word choice, "Yes, ma'am."

"Alex," Martha began, "no matter how old you get or how big you think you are, respect your momma." Martha smiled and winked. Alex nodded with a large smile.

"How did you sleep last night?" Paul asked Alex.

"It was hard to fall asleep. But Mom came into my room, and I fell asleep in her arms. It was like when I was little. When I would get scared. She always knew how to calm me down."

"Moms have that power, ya knows. God gave us superpowers. Like being able to see out the back of our heads when you are doing something you are not supposed to. We know when you are hurting even when you try to hide it," Martha commented. "A lot of people try to protect us from their hurts, but that is what we are here for. We are here for you." Martha turned to Paul.

"Yes, ma'am, Mom," Paul answered.

"Alex, can you…or will you tell us how you were feeling last night when Colton came here?" Martha asked.

Alex sat there for a few minutes sipping his orange juice. "It's okay if you don't want to. I do not want you to feel forced." Martha acknowledged Alex's difficulty in finding the words he wanted.

Alex nodded. "Paul, are you okay? This must be difficult for you?"

Martha turned her attention to her son. Paul had sat down at the table with his coffee. "Yes, ma'am. I am struggling. And…to be honest, I am not sure exactly why but do at the same time." Martha reached out with her hand to her son's. "Paul, you stepped in as a father figure and now you are not sure how you fit in this now. Now that Colton is back in the picture."

Alex sat in silence listening to Martha calm her son's nerves about the situation now before him. He could not understand (1) why they were talking like this in front of him. Most of the time he had to eavesdrop for good stuff like this. (2) He wasn't sure how to react to Paul because he didn't want to hurt him. (3) How Martha understood all this so well and why was he so confused. She was old.

"Mom, when Carter died, I died. Melony tried. I tried. But neither of us knew how to recover. When she came to the ceremony… and spoke those beautiful words to me, to the crowd, I had no idea. I had no idea that she felt that way. Then I felt so bad that I failed her. When Alex tried to rob me, all I saw was Carter. I do not understand how, but I saw Carter." Alex listened intently. "I had been helping from the sidelines when I could for years when I first encountered them. I guess I adopted Alex."

Paul turned to Alex and smiled. "Now I…now I don't know how to feel."

"Paul," Alex began, "can I ask you a question?"

"Sure, son," Paul answered. "Why me and Mom? There were lots of people in that area that could have used help. Why did you choose us?" Alex sat, staring at Paul with confused concern in his eyes.

"I don't know exactly. When you and your mom moved in, I saw the typical single-parent family you hear about. Lots of different thoughts ran through my mind about you two. At first, I just noticed you in the distance, but soon it became very noticeable to me that you both were struggling. It was only me, so I had some extra. I did not want a relationship of any kind. I was still wallowing in my own grief. Maybe I did see Carter in you from the beginning, and it did not register until you tried to rob me. All I know is that it hit me like a ton of bricks that I was to help you from a distance." Paul stopped for a moment, reflecting on this journey. Then he giggled a little. "Ya know, you almost caught me one time. You almost caught me leaving the groceries. I think you might have been about ten or eleven. School let out early, and you showed up just as I was about to go up on your porch."

Paul started laughing. "I had to do a quick about-face and take all those groceries to the store."

Alex's eyes lit up. "I remember that. I remember that. I remember that I was thinking you were a weird old guy. Then you took the food inside your shop, and I was like, 'Why is he doing that?' I was right." Alex chuckled. "You are a weird old guy."

Martha started laughing. Paul and Alex traded barbs for a while. Martha was happy that the two of them had found each other. They were going to need each other to get through this ordeal with Colton.

"Mom," Paul started, "thank you for hosting us. I am embarrassed about how I acted and how I shut you out. Do you forgive me?"

"Paul, you are my son. There is no forgiveness needed. You were hurting and did what you thought you needed to. The best part of it all, you found Alex. And without even realizing it, Alex saved you before you ever saved him." Martha and Paul hugged, then she excused herself to begin brunch.

"Ms. Martha," Alex spoke up, "I am happy you let us stay here. Thank you."

"You are quite welcome, young man. Will you come in the kitchen and help me?" Martha asked. "Yes, ma'am."

The two of them left Paul with his coffee and the morning newspaper. He wasn't really reading it, just kind of looking at the pictures and the words.

"Good morning, Paul." Kim appeared from the hallway. "Can I get you a cup of coffee?"

Paul asked as he stood to pull out a chair for her. "Yes, please. I fell asleep on the floor with Alex last night. But when I woke up, I was in his bed, and he was nowhere to be found."

Paul excused himself and went to the kitchen. He advised the other two that Kim was up and that somehow, she was in bed instead of the floor where she fell asleep. Alex smiled and went back to helping Martha. All of a sudden, Alex had found peace, and it was in the kitchen of all places, with Martha.

Paul delivered the cup of coffee to Kim. The two of them sat and talked and listened to Alex goad Martha then Alex yelp when Martha set him straight. Kim smiled. "Paul, your family is beautiful and kind. Thank you." Kim leaned over and gave Paul a kiss on the cheek. He blushed then tipped his imaginary hat with a wink of an eye.

"Kim, can I ask you a question?"

"Sure, what is it?"

"What went through your mind when you saw Colton...I mean Cole."

"To be honest, I have dreamed of this day. I have dreamed of a day when Alex could meet his father. I knew, at least I thought I knew, it was impossible, but when I saw him"—she paused—"I knew God had answered my prayers. He must have had his reasons for what he did. Protecting me from something. But it does not matter. I have him back, even if it is just at a distance. I have him back. It is Alex I am worried about. And you. You Paul. You two have such a bond. He is torn between the possibilities of having his dad that he never knew and the man who became his dad when he most needed one. Then you. Yes, I see you." Kim smiled at Paul. She could see the tears welling up. So she knew a "smart" remark was soon to be here.

"Kim, Mom said it best. I came to your aid long ago because Alex became my Carter. Then I became his dad when he was trying to find himself. You are right. We are both torn, but please understand, I only want to help. I do not want to be in the way. I can be uncle or grandpa if you like...I prefer uncle," he said with a smile.

Mary knocked on Colton's door. "Colton, are you awake?"

It was almost nine, and she had not seen him emerge from his room yet. Tim and Mary had been up for a couple of hours now. They had just about polished off one pot of coffee and discussed every possible topic they could think of. Lest the one they really wanted to talk about, Colton and Kim.

"Colton, are you up? It is 9:00 a.m. You might want to think about getting up soon. We need to be at Martha's by eleven." Mary tried again. There was no answer. Not wanting to invade his privacy, but thinking he just might not hear her, she cracked the door and saw that his bed had not been slept in. "Tim!"

"Colton is not in his room." Tim rushed down the hallway to Mary; she swung open the door. All his things were still there, but his bed looked like he had not been in it all night. "Tim, go to the brook. See if he slept down there." Tim agreed. He slid on his shoes and a light jacket then headed off to the brook. Along the way, he prayed that he would find Colton, and everything would be okay.

Tim made it to the brook, where he found Colton asleep on the bridge. "Hey…hey…Colton, wake up." Tim gently nudged him. Colton jolted and drew back. When his eyes had focused, he saw Tim standing over him. "Easy tiger, I ain't gonna hurt you." Tim stepped back. Colton dropped his hands and pushed himself up into a seated position. "Sorry."

"No worries, kiddo. Why did you sleep out here?" Rubbing his eyes and trying to stretch out his aching muscles, Colton explained that he was just thinking, praying, and crying a lot. "Tim, I am a bad man. I left the woman I love to raise a child without a father. What kind of a man does that?" Still stretching, Colton began and started telling Tim his story—from how he met Kim, how they fell in love, how he was going to marry her. They were going to be together forever. Then…he paused for a moment. Then his last deployment when his friends Michael, James, and Scott were killed by a roadside bomb. How he had been detailed that day to command and how guilty he feels for not being dead too. Colton spilled every one of his demons to Tim. Tim sat down beside him and listened.

"Tim"—Colton was wiping his face clean—"Tim, I did make a decision though last night. I remember you telling me about your talk with your grandson while you were in a coma. That he wanted to be like the squirrel. To jump fearlessly. Tim, I want to be that squirrel. I want to jump fearlessly."

"Colton, can I ask you a question. Have the voices returned?"

With a puzzled look, "How did you know?"

"I believe that you can be that squirrel. I believe that you were meant to be that squirrel. I also know that as long as the hawk is circling within you, you are in danger of falling to him. The enemy will take many forms. He will even go after Alex. Are you prepared to hear the hate and fear from your son? It is going to hurt. Are you prepared for that attack?"

The two men sat on the bridge in silence as Colton fed off Tim's words. Just then, the screech of a hawk was heard in the trees above. Colton looked at Tim and Tim at him. With amazement in their eyes, a cool breeze blew through the trees. It was slightly cool but refreshing. Not harsh, but gentle, and the atmosphere went from startled to calm.

"Tim, was that God?"

Not quite sure how to answer him, Tim agreed, and they headed for the house. While Colton was in the shower, Tim told Mary about the hawk and breeze. She explained that as soon as Tim left for the brook, she began praying. She felt something was slightly off then claimed God's promises to never leave them. After that, she felt at ease, and it wasn't long after that, the two of them exited the woods. Shaking his head, Tim hugged Mary and whispered, "I don't know if I will ever understand him."

Mary giggled and replied, "You already do. I love you."

Chapter Seventeen

Tim, Mary, and Colton loaded up into the car and headed for Martha's. The ride was extremely quiet. Too quiet. Eerie quiet. Everyone seemed to be too scared to say anything.

"Arrrrrrrgggggghhhhhhhhhhhhhh!" Colton launched a hideous loud yell from the back seat. Mary jumped in her seat. Tim hit the brakes hard and swerved to the side of the road. Both of them jolted around to see what was wrong with Colton, only to find him with a cheesy grin on his face. "Tension breaker, I feel better now… don't you?" At that point, the three of them broke into uncontrollable laughter.

Pulling up to Martha's, Colton's laughter ceased a little, and he could feel the nerves inside him starting to fester. Mary turned to him and reassured that it was going to be all right. Tim reminded him that he was the squirrel. He was leaping with faith that he would land on the tree limb before him…safely. He reminded him of the chipmunk, another story he had told him, and that all he had to do was seek out the best path. That path was with God leading. He needed to be bold and not be intimidated by the brook or the empty air between branches. Then Tim reminded him that the worst thing that could happen is that he would fall in the brook, have to take a bath, and then he would no longer smell like a turd. The three chuckled and went into the house.

Walking in, Tim made a grand announcement about the "best" son was here to have brunch with the "best" mom ever. Before anyone could comment, Alex popped off. "Too late…I am here. I am the best son and now grandson to the best two ladies ever. Take a seat, old man." Paul spit out his coffee, and Kim told Alex to apologize, though she, too, was laughing.

Alex helped Martha set the table. They had made a spread to feed the town. They had scrambled eggs, toast, sausage, bacon, ham, waffles, pancakes, fresh fruit, coffee, tea, milk, and orange juice. After they had finished, Tim asked, "What? No biscuits and gravy?" Martha looked at Tim with a mother's look and replied, "There's the kitchen, have at it. My breakfast is getting cold." Alex sighed out an "Oooooooooh." Tim smiled and declined the offer. Martha sat at the head of the table. To her right was Mary, Tim, and Colton. Paul was at the other end, followed by Kim then Alex. "Paul, will you say the blessing…no—" Martha stopped in midsentence. "Alex, would you do me a favor sir, and say the blessing over breakfast?" Silence fell over the table. Alex agreed.

"Father in heaven, thank you for this meal. Thank you for Ms. Martha and her hospitality. Thank you for bringing us here. Please bless this meal. And God. Thank you for making my mom smile again. In Jesus's name we pray…amen."

Alex looked at Martha. "Was that okay?"

She replied with loving eyes and a nod of her head.

Diligently, Paul and Tim began their antics at the table. They were fighting over every little thing. You would have thought that they were seven again. Martha cleared her throat, and the two toned it down slightly. Colton patiently waited for each item to meet his end. Everyone filled their plates, and there was a nice quiet meal in progress when all of a sudden, there was a shift in the atmosphere. There appeared an awkwardness. The air was stiff. The mood was solemn.

Martha stood and retreated to the kitchen. She had finished her meal and took her dishes to the sink. She was gone for a bit when all of a sudden, out of nowhere, there came a barrage of mini marshmallows. From the kitchen doorway, she began pelting everyone. Never having seen this side of their mother, Tim and Paul sat confused. Alex began laughing.

Martha then started shouting out, "Begone in the name of Pilsbury. Begone, you negative spirits. Begone, you evildoers of hiding the sprinkles." As they realized that she was trying to get everyone to lighten up, Tim grabbed the salt and began to salt everyone so that they would be flavorful. Without hesitation, Mary picked up pieces of bread, tossed it in the air, and called it to life. Paul was certain that they had all gone mad, but it looked like too much fun, so he searched a way to join in. Out of the corner of his eye, he saw a spray bottle near one of Martha's plants and began to baptize everyone in name of biscuits and gravy. Kim and Colton just took cover under the table; however, Alex was not about to let them get away. Within minutes, everyone was laughing, and the room was a mess. This was worse than any food fight Alex had ever seen.

Never in all their life had Tim and Paul seen their mother react in such a way. She had always been proper and stern with the rules. She loved them and they played, but a food fight…oh, that would have gotten them a trip to the shed in a heartbeat. With everyone laughing hysterically at the nonsense that just ensued, Tim called out, "Mom…have you lost your mind? I love it if you have."

Martha resumed her seat at the head of the table and began to drink her coffee as though nothing had happened. With puzzled bewilderment, each person resumed their seat cautiously, still reeling in laughter. Once everyone was seated, Martha answered, "Children—yes, you are all children. There was a spirit that had been trying to take over this house for the last two or three days. I won't allow it. I know you all have your 'manners' in gear to be polite and respectful to my house. The spirit knows this. Now, I am going to exert my mother's right and clear the air. I have your attention now. Don't I?"

They all giggled out a "Yes, ma'am."

She continued, "Normally I would not involve myself in such personal matters as these. This is going to take a lot of time for the healing to take place. But I can feel it starting already. There are lots of questions. There is a lot of gray area. Colton, I will not ask. It is not my place, but you will need to do a lot of explaining. Not only to Kim but also to Alex. It is no one else's business unless you wish to share." Martha looked straight at Paul. "Alex, you are hurting and confused. I am a strong and faithful woman of God. I know that the spirits have been seeking you out. They know you are the target to get the most leverage. I want you to know that everything happens for a reason. There is a reason that Colton lied. There is a reason that Paul saw you when you were little. There is a reason that Tim had his accident. There is a reason that Colton found Mary. There is a reason I started the food fight." She stopped for a moment and took a drink of her tea. "Paul, you are battling a slew of emotions. Right now, you and Tim are wondering if your mother is in her right mind. Both of you, do you remember the time at the beach when you those older boys were messing with you, and I made you go apologize to them? You both looked at me like I was crazy. Then I purchased four ice creams. One for each of you and one for them. You again looked at me like I was crazy. As the day went on, do you remember what happened?"

Tim answered, "We all ended up playing together and having a great time."

"That's right. What you didn't know is that those two boys were from abusive parents. No one had shown them love. When we showed them love, they returned the kindness. Alex, you have to understand, there are some things that you and Paul are going to relate to that Colton will not. But in turn, there is a path for you and Colton as well. It is going to be difficult. It is going to be emotional. The spirit is not going to let up. He is going to go after you both. Everything is not going to be worked out this week while you are here. It may take years for it to all work out. It may never be completely worked out. But as long as you never stop working on it, love will prevail. Children, we have but one God. He loves us no matter what we have done. Believe it or not, I have not always been this faithful. I have not always been this hospitable. There are many things in my past that even my boys do not know. I promise you that forgiveness does not give the offender a free pass for their actions, but it does give you a free pass to heal. Now I have one last thing to say, and I expect you all to comply with my request. First, Mary, will you stay and help me clean up? Second, Tim and Paul, I would like you two to disappear and have some quality time together as brothers. Lastly, I would like you three to go to the park, it is a beautiful day. I want you to go there and have an open discussion and start the healing process. Tomorrow is church, and I expect all of you to be there."

Everyone accepted Martha's commentary and requests. They were silenced with her sincerity and outpouring of love. Never had even Tim or Paul heard their mother speak in such a manner. The boys headed out to Tim's shop to build or break something, they had not quite decided. Mary began clearing the table. Alex asked Martha for a moment of her time.

The two of them stepped out to the back patio and closed the doors behind them. "Ms. Martha," Alex began. "I am scared. I do not want to know him, but I do at the same time. How could he not want to be with my mom if they were so much in love?" Martha reached over and gave Alex a big grandma-type hug. "Son, these are questions that only he can answer. I know you are scared. But you know what else?" Alex shook his head no. "I know that God brought Colton here for a reason. I know that God brought Paul to you for a reason. I know that you all are here for a reason. I believe that the reason is to show that all relationships can be healed, if given a chance." Alex pulled away and looked her in the eye. "You were right, you know. I do hear voices. They are not nice. They want me to hate him, but I can't because he makes Mom smile. How can I hate someone who makes her smile?"

Martha smiled and replied, "Don't hate Alex. That is a waste of energy. It does no one any good at all. Give Colton a chance. You are not going to lose Paul if you accept Colton. I know my son. He is stuck on you like glue. He is not going anywhere. I promise. The two of them returned to the house. Colton and Kim had started helping Mary clean up the disaster zone. Tim and Paul took their release from chores seriously and bolted as soon as Martha cleared the back door. They were not taking any chances of her changing her mind.

Martha reiterated what she wanted from the three of them. They were to go to the park and talk. There were plenty of pavilions there where they could sit and get to know each other. There were a few trails they could hike if they desired. The idea was to start the rebuilding of this relationship. With simple steps of conversation. They each bid a "Yes, ma'am" and left for the park.

Once Martha saw that the three had gotten down the sidewalk a piece, she told Mary to stop cleaning and come sit a spell in the front room. She told her the mess was not going anywhere, and since no one was brave enough to spray syrup, they were going to be just fine in the cleaning.

Each grabbed a spot of tea and retired to the sitting room. They sat in silence for a good little while when Mary broke the silence with a not-so-ladylike burp. Martha nearly spewed her tea and gave the mannered "excuse you." The two giggled like teenage girls.

"Mary, do you understand why I started the food fight?"

With a smirky smile, she replied, "Actually, I do. I was trying to figure out a way to help them all come together but did not know how to start a conversation. The next thing I know, I am taking a marshmallow to the side of the head."

Martha smiled as she took another sip of tea. "Mary, I did not sleep well last night. I could feel the tension in the air. I prayed that God would use me to open the dialogue gate. I had a dream that was quite odd. Nothing like this has ever crossed my mind. God spoke to me in the story of Peter and the unclean food. I wasn't really sure what he was talking about until this morning when Alex and I were working on brunch. He had told me about a time when he was at the restaurant with his mom after school and some grown-ups got into a fight, and out of nowhere, he got hit with a meatball. While he was telling the story, God reminded me of the dream. I decided to wait and see how conversations were going to flow and when they really didn't because of the obvious elephant in the room, I went to see what I had that was going to cause the least amount of damage." Mary and she started laughing at the sight of marshmallows flying through this prim and proper home.

"Well, you certainly know how to get everyone's attention."

Mary giggled. "That is for sure. But to be honest, I think I needed that release more than anyone in the room. Always being the one in control gets tiring. And to be absolutely clear, I just wish I could have gotten on film the look on Tim and Paul's faces as I started winging marshmallows. It was priceless from my vantage point."

The ladies continued their conversation, laughing and reliving each point of the chaos. They agreed that Satan must be scratching his head while Jesus and the apostles were enjoying the show.

Tim and Paul had escaped as soon as Martha had told them to get lost. They were not sure what had come over their mother, but this was one time they were not going to question her. That dining room was a disaster—marshmallows, salt, bread all soaked in plant water. Hilarious for sure, but nonetheless a mess.

"What on Earth came over *your* mother?" Paul exclaimed.

"*My* mother. Like she did not give birth to you too?" Tim replied in a most sarcastic tone. "I have no idea but feel great. To know that she has this kind of side, that is wonderful. However, I am not sure I want to know 'why' this side came out." Tim giggled.

The boys pulled into the drive and decided it was a good time to race to the shop. Just as they both got out of the car, Paul hit the ground. Tim was a good fifty feet in the lead. Paul yelled out in pain as if he had twisted his ankle getting out of the car. Tim stopped and came back to help him up, making wise cracks about his age and how fragile he was now that he was old. Just as Tim got to Paul and helped him to his feet, Paul shoved Tim into the car and took off running. Tim regained his balance, and the race was on. Paul knew that Tim was going to win straight out of the gate but had to make it a bit more challenging. The two felt as though they were boys again and, for some unknown conscious reason, decided to act like it as well. Just as Tim caught back up with Paul, he wrapped his arms around his waist, thrusting him to the ground in a good old-fashioned tackle. Both men let out a hearty lung of air. They rolled apart from each other, and once they got some air back to speak, recited together that the tackle probably was not a very smart idea. However, that did not stop them from continuing to hobble race to the shop.

When they got to the shop, they were both laughing so hard that they could barely stand up. Inside, Paul found a bench, and Tim got them each a bottle of water. The two sat and talked about how each of them cheated and that they each had won. After all the bragging had ceased, Paul asked, "Tim, can I ask you a question? About Cole or Colton?" Seeing how serious Paul was in his question, Tim forewent the desire to call him out on how many questions he was actually asking. "Sure. Go for it."

Paul took another drink of his water and asked, "Is he a good guy? I don't want Kim or Alex to get hurt."

Tim proceeded to explain to Paul how Colton came into their lives. That he was actually a school chum of Mary's. "And by chance happened onto our property one night. Fast forward, when we met up again, Mary recognized him and after some prayerful consideration, we invited him to stay with us. There were some secrets, we knew, but did not anticipate this. I think he has been with us now for about a year, maybe a little longer. He got a job as the maintenance guy at the church. He pays a little rent, and we give a little peace. There is a brook toward the back of the property that we go to and sit on the bridge when we need to get away and think, he likes to spend time out there. I shared with him my encounter with the chasm in my mind and the stories that my dream state grandson and I had. I explained how I was learning to accept and follow God, also trying to encourage him to do the same. Since he has gotten settled, he seems to have less issues with haunting demons of his past."

The two brothers sat and talked well into the late afternoon about just about everything under the sun. They talked about Tim's close encounter with death. They talked about how their father had died. They talked about how their mother never seemed to waver in the toughest of times. They talked more about Carter and Melony. They talked about every topic that could possibly come up. They even delved into politics for a short while. At the end of the day, the brothers were closer than they had been in years.

"Show me this brook you were talking about," Paul commanded. "Why, yes, sir, I sure will, sir. Right now, sir. Whatever you command, sir." Tim snapped to attention and began to march. The two men began to wrestle and play around again. They got about halfway down the path with Tim grabbed up a clump of dirt and smearing it on Paul's arm promptly shouted, "YOU'RE A TURD!"

Tim hit the ground on one knee and started laughing. It took Paul a moment to remember the conversation covering the story Tiny Tim told when Tim was in a coma. The two started laughing and Paul stated that he guessed he would have to take a bath now. First one in years.

When they got to the brook, they found a spot to sit and dangle their legs. Tim told of an adventure of Tiny and him where Tiny asked Tim if he was mad at God and if Grandma was happy. Tim told it as if it had happened yesterday. Sitting on the bridge, Paul listened to his brother regale in detail the inquisitive nature of his grandson. The sincerity of his query. The love in his heart. "Paul, Carter loves you. He is at peace. Melony loves you too. She has kept in touch with us on occasion. She—" Tim stopped for a moment. Paul's eyes were fixed on Tim. "She wants to talk, but she is not sure how to approach you. When she found out that you were getting that award, her heart filled with joy. She told us—that is how we found out. Truth be told." Tears began to flow down Paul's cheek. "I miss her. I have wanted to talk to her on many occasions but could not find the courage to knock on her door."

Tim explained to Paul the stories of the squirrel and the chipmunk that he had told Tiny and Colton. He encouraged his brother to be like the squirrel: Leap out in faith and contact her so that they can have complete healing. That doesn't mean that they get remarried or even date; but they do need to talk, cry, shout, and forgive. Paul stated that he would look her up as soon as he got home and promised that he would do his part to start the healing. He still loved her…and hoped that she loved him enough to talk.

Chapter Eighteen

As Colton, Kim, and Alex left Martha's home, the mood was light and full of fun. The three of them walked together, almost family like. They had barely cleared the yard when Alex looked at Colton and simply asked, "Why?"

Kim began to intervene when Colton stopped her. "Kim, it's a fair and important question. He deserves an honest answer. As do you. I have a lot of explaining to do. But if I might ask, can we wait until we get to the park and sit down. I want my words to be clear and make sense. I am afraid that if I try to walk and talk, I will not be able to explain myself clearly." Kim looked at Alex with her mother's eyes, and he agreed.

The park was only three blocks away from Martha's house. They walked in silence, but the atmosphere was congealed in good humor. Right before they got to the park, Alex raised his hands, laid them firmly on their shoulders, and shouted, "Be healed in the name of Pilsbury." At the time he shouted it, a passerby stopped and stared. That, in turn, created uncontrollable laughter from the three. As the stranger looked at them even harder, Kim called out, "Incoming," and they pretended to take cover from Martha's assault. This made the stranger eagerly pass with vengeance. He was certain they were crazy.

Outside the park was a small convenience store. Colton went inside to grab a couple of waters for each of them. All the pavilions were free except one in the front where the kids were playing superheroes. They took seats around the tables. Colton opened his water, took a solid drink, then a deep breath.

"First," he started, "first, I want to thank you for waiting to the park before asking for answers. I have been thinking about you"—he looked at Kim—"for a long time. Had I known about you"—he turned to Alex—"I would have pressed to get better faster…I think." Colton stopped and thought about how that sounded. "Let me try this again because I just put both my feet in my mouth, and I did not realize I could do that." Colton took a breath. "Okay, let me try this again. I am going to start from the beginning and try to explain why I did what I did. Once you know the meaning, then you can make your choice of if you want to talk to me or see me ever again."

An ominous whisper blew through the pavilion. "*Lies.*" The voice curled around Alex's ears, like a moth to a flame. "*Lies.*" The whisper gently caressed the back of his neck. "*Lies. Everything he says is lies.*"

In Alex's mind, he began to predict the story he was about to be told. He wanted to know if he could read this guy and if he was a threat. His instinct to protect his mother again caused his body to tense. As he felt that tension, he remembered what Martha had said about the demons targeting him. He needed to stay focused. He needed to block them out. The only thing he could think of was the Lord's prayer. He didn't want to say in his head; he wanted to be heard, so he interrupted Colton and asked if he could say a prayer before Colton began. Confused, Kim looked at her son as if he were an alien, and Colton was relieved for a few more minutes to compose himself. Alex began: "Our father, who art in heaven, hallowed by thy name, your kingdom come, your will be done on earth as it is in heaven. Give us this day our daily bread. Forgive us our debts, as we also have forgiven our debtors. And lead us not into temptation but deliver us from the evil one. For thine is the kingdom and the power and glory forever. Amen." When Alex had finished, the evil spirit had left, and he could now focus on what Colton had to say. In his mind, he gave thanks to God for Martha and her words, so that he knew what he was dealing with.

"Alex, that was wonderful. Thank you for that prayer. I needed that boost of energy." Colton looked at Alex with sincerity in his eyes. Kim was astonished that Alex knew that prayer. Refocusing on what Colton had to say, Kim and Alex sat silently. "When I left on deployment the last time, I lost a lot of good friends. One day, I will tell you all about them if you like, but for now, know that when they died, I felt very guilty." Colton told his story from start to finish. He explained that after he returned to the States, he was not the same person, and he knew that he would be a danger to Kim. He had to get his own mind and heart in the right place if he was ever going to be any good to anyone. At the time he sent the letter, he did not believe that he would ever be that person and wanted Kim to be free to make a life for herself. He told of the many voices he could hear in his head. He told of the many places where he had been beat up for simply being there. He told of the countless times he was arrested for sleeping—on a bench or under a tree. He had spent many nights in homeless shelters only to be beaten and robbed there too. He was charged twice with aggravated assault. One time when someone woke him up, he was in the middle of a nightmare about the war. He came up defending himself, breaking the person's nose and collarbone. The second time he was having a very bad day when a young pompous college kid decided he was going to show "him" a lesson. That kid landed in the hospital for about two weeks. The first case was dismissed. The second case was lessoned in a plea deal with the understanding that he would leave the area and not return. "I have used alcohol on a few occasions to forget…but it never worked. All it did was give me a massive headache."

Colton continued to explain the last seventeen years. He did not leave any details out. As he told everything, he explained everything the way he thought, the way he was thinking, what he deduced to be the best course of action. The conversation took well over three hours to deliver. He was determined to set the record straight and see what happened next. When he had concluded his life history, he realized that they were all out of water. He had drunk his and one of Kim's. He excused himself to go back to the convenience store and retrieve more water and a snack. He was in need for a snack. He asked Alex if he would like to join him; however, Alex declined. Colton understood and went to the store alone.

"Mom," Alex began, "do you believe him?"

Kim sat silently processing all that she had heard. The pain that he endured. The suffering he felt. The shame and guilt that he bore. Now, knowing that he abandoned his son and love, the added guilt that must be on his shoulders. Kim's only thought was she needed to help her Cole. He needed her, and she was not going to abandon him.

"Alex, I do. I do believe him. And I do understand why he did what he did. I may disagree with him and wish that he would have come to me in the beginning, but I know his heart. He knew he could not be a husband to me the way he felt I deserved. Now hearing his story, he would not have been a good father for you either. Though we had it rough, we had each other. Yes, he chose to have no one, but no one should have no one…regardless of their choices. God led him to Tim and Mary. God led you to Paul. We are meant to work this out."

Alex sat and listened to his mother closely. Even in his rebellious phase, she was always there for him. He was never alone. Even when he "felt" he was, he knew his mother loved him completely. The voices, though quieter, were still swirling around him like sweat bees in the summertime. They were there, not really doing anything, just being annoying. Slight whispers of deception and dishonesty. Just loud enough and close enough to want to swat them away.

Colton returned with the water, a couple of sodas, and a bag full of chips and candy. "I wasn't sure what you all liked, so I just kind of got a little of everything." The three laughed, and Alex popped off, "What? No marshmallows?" Colton smiled, and Kim noticed that her son was going to give this a try. He did not act like this with those who did not have a chance.

"May I ask you a question, Alex?" Colton began.

Inquisitively, Alex replied, "Sure?"

"Is there anything you would like to ask me specifically? Maybe something I did not say or do. Something that doesn't fit right with you. Please ask." Colton popped open soda and a bag of chocolate candy.

Alex studied his questions and then replied, "Yes. I have a few questions. I keep hearing voices that tell me not to believe you, that you are lying, and this is all a game. Now I don't know if it is a game or not. I have not figured that out yet. But what I cannot make sense of is this: If you truly loved my mother so much that you left to protect her, why did you not search for her when you started getting better? I do not understand how a man who is determined to protect and love would not want to—" Alex stopped because he could feel his temper growing. He was hurt. He was confused. The voices were getting louder again. Once he composed himself again, he continued, "Even if you did not want to take a chance to hurt her, you could have looked for her and sent her money anonymously. Like Paul did with the groceries. She would never had known it was you and you would still have been taking care of her."

Colton sat and listened to the love Alex had for his mother. The admiration and respect she had earned in his eyes. He had no answer that would satisfy Alex's questions. "Sir, all I can do is offer an apology. No answer will suffice. Nothing is going to satisfy you as an answer. I was selfish, which I admitted. I did what I did thinking I was protecting. Once I sent the letter, I knew I had no right to intrude on her life. So the few times it did cross my mind to seek your mother out, I reminded myself that I made a choice, and I was going to live with that choice the rest of my life. Now...that being said, I am just as sorry that I did not seek her out. If I had, I would have learned about you. Growing up without a father is difficult. I had one and still feel as though I did not. I am not sure what I would have done differently, but I would like to think I would have. I truly wish I had a better answer for you. You are entitled to one."

Listening closely to their conversation, Kim heard two men talking as men...not as boys positioning for power. She was proud of her son for not releasing all his emotions and she was proud of Cole for opening his heart to them both.

"Cole...Colton...first...which do you prefer?" Kim started.

"Kim, I will always be your Cole."

"Fine, Cole." She took a drink of her water. "Now I am going to share my story." She looked at Alex. "Some of it you know because you lived through it, but some you do not. Please do not interrupt."

Both gentlemen sat silently as Kim began to speak. "About two years ago, you were in Capers, weren't you?"

Cole replied, "Uh, yes, how did you know?"

Tears welling up in her eyes, she continued, "I knew it then, but did not know what to do. So I said nothing, and we continued on our way. I saw you against the wall of the train station. You were sitting with your back against the wall, your pack underneath your bent legs, minding your own business, just sitting inside out of the rain. A station manager came and told you to move along. You asked for a little more time to rest, they granted it, but gave you a deadline to get out of the station. My eyes fixed on you from a distance. My heart raced. I wanted to approach you, but I knew you were dead. That this must have been a doppelganger. Your voice and your mannerisms gave you away. I reasoned that I 'wanted' it to be you, so I 'made' it you, but you were gone, and I needed to keep walking. And I did. Our eyes did lock for a second, but I quickly broke contact and moved on to catch our train." Kim paused for a moment.

Colton reflected back to the train station. That incident she was talking about. He was ashamed that he did not recognize her. Probably because she had a teenage son with her, and it never crossed his mind that it could be her. Alex remembered that trip because he got food poisoning on the train, and all he wanted to do was get home and sleep.

"That entire trip home, I wondered if that could be you. But then rationality kicked in, and I left it as 'a wish' for the impossible." Another pause and drink of water. "Fast forward. When I was shown the picture of you from Tim and Mary. I was in shock. A multitude of questions flooded my mind. I wanted to be angry with you, but all I could do was rejoice in my heart. You need to know that when I found out I was pregnant with Alex, it was the happiest day of my life. When I found out that you were gone was the saddest. But as I watched Alex grow up, I watched you regain life. I never attempted to find a father for Alex. I decided that I would use your memory to father for him. In the early years, it was okay, but as he became a man, he went the 'hard' way. Thankfully, Paul was there to guide him. I didn't know Paul. Never laid eyes on him before that I knew of. I am truly thankful for a man who stepped into my…our son's life to help him find his way." Kim was beginning to tear up. Her voice was cracking. Her confidence and strength were failing. Her agony of the "loss" of Cole was creeping up and like a monsoon tidal wave. No longer could she control her emotions.

"You!" Kim raised her voice. "You, you have no idea the pain I suffered because of your disappearance. I am angry with you. Part of me wants to tell you that you made your choice, now deal with it. take my son and leave forever." Tears were flowing steadily from her eyes; Colton absorbed her words and tears of embarrassment and failure flowed as quickly. Alex sat and respected the moment. He so wanted to get involved and defend his mother but knew that he had to remain silent.

"Kim," Colton said softly. She raised her finger to him in a motion of him to wait and be silent for her to finish. "You hurt me. You hurt me when you did not trust me to help you. After all we went through together, the fights with your dad, the destruction of your mom. I never left your side. Why…why would you think that I would leave your side in the most devastating time of your life…the loss of your only family…Cole…I love you."

The evening was set; the three of them continued to have an open discussion about everything. No stone was left unturned. Apologies were issued and accepted. As the sun began to sink below the horizon, the bag of goodies was all but gone. Dinner was not even an idea. The three walked back to Martha's. Exhausted from the emotional strain of the day. But…free of secrets.

Chapter Nineteen

"Good morning to everyone. Welcome. We here are encouraged to see so many beautiful and bright faces. To the newcomers, *welcome*. We pray that this service will move you in ways that you were not expecting. We are a family here and wish everyone to feel welcome. Now, a little different this morning, I want to start off this morning with the Lord's prayer. Please join me as we recited his prayer." This was Tom's opening to service.

"Our Father, who art in in heaven..." In unison, everyone seemingly recited.

"Yes," a deep and commanding voice replied.

The church fell silent. Tom stopped, stuttered a bit, and began again.

"Our Father who art in heaven. Hallowed be thy name."

"Yes, I heard you the first time. How can I help you today?"

Tom stopped. Shock and awe appeared on his face. Silence was all about the congregation. Tim and Mary were staring at each other. Alex tried to speak, but Kim shhh-ed him. Colton's jaw was open. The kids were all present, except for Jon, who had to work for a call in. Everyone was silent.

"Who is this?" Tom commanded. "Show yourself."

"Tom, you called me. You know who I am. Why do I need to show myself?"

"Mary, the hair...on...my neck" Tim whispered. Mary waived him off.

"God?" Tom questioned.

"Is that not who you called upon. Your Father in heaven?"

"Um…yes. But—"

"You called for me, but now you question when I arrive. Do you not believe in the power of prayer, Tom? Do you not have faith that I hear your cries? Does my word not say where two or more are gathered, I am there? Why are you so surprised."

"Father…" exasperated and embarrassed. Tom bowed his head.

"Yes, Tom."

"Will you…will you listen to us now, though we have felt doubt?"

"Of course. Please continue."

Regrouping his thoughts. "Please pray with me for the Father. Our Father who art in heaven. Hallowed by thy name. Thy kingdom come, thy will be done on earth as it is in heaven."

"Excuse me. May I interrupt here for just a second. Do you really mean it?"

Confused, Tom asked "Lord?"

"Do you really mean my will be done here on earth as it is in heaven?"

"Yes, Lord."

"Mary, I am confused. What is going on?" Tim continued to try and get her attention. "Is that really God?"

Tom stuttered, "Lord, what do you mean? Of course, we are here for your will."

"Are you now? Can I ask you why the donations have not gone out to the homeless shelter yet? You prayed for abundance, you received abundance, yet the funds remain in your coffer. Whose will is that? Building little interest nest egg, are we? Will that interest also be headed to the shelter? Or will it stay in the coffer?"

"Uh…mmmmmm. I have no answer for you."

"Continue with your prayer. The voices are music to my ears.

Clearing his throat, Tom continued, "Give us this day our daily bread. Forgive us our trespasses as we forgive those who trespass against us."

"Sorry to interrupt, I have another question. Actually two: (1) How much bread do you need to be sustained, and (2) are you forgiving others as I forgive you or are you holding on to their mistakes?"

"Lord? I have plenty. I forgive. I don't understand."

"Tom, if you have plenty, then why the side hustle? If you are content with my blessings, why do you have another job? As far as forgiving, can you tell me about Doug? And Kathy? And Pete…"

"Okay, Lord. Okay. I get it. But they really hurt me. You know what they did. How can I forgive them for that?"

"Tom, I forgave you, didn't I? But we will continue that conversation in private, please continue the praying. This is music to me. I love the sound of my children's voices speaking to me."

Almost fearful of finishing his prayer. Tom continued, "And lead us not into temptation, but deliver us from the evil one. For thine is the kingdom, the power and the glory forever, amen."

Stillness fell over the sanctuary. What was the voice going to say?" Tom paused a moment then continued, "Good morning, everyone. Thank you for reciting the Lord's prayer with me today. As you may have noticed, we had an honored guest." A gasp went about the room. "No, that was not God…that was Jon. I enlisted Jon to help me with this experiment. I believe it was a success."

Murmurs circulated the room. Some were angry and embarrassed. Some were amused. Some…well, they took the beginning of the lesson to heart.

"Again, welcome to all newcomers. Today we are going to start off our song worship with a favorite children's song, 'Jesus Loves Me.'"

The piano began to play, and the auditorium exploded in joyful sounds. The words could be heard blocks away and the doors to the church were closed. As the song concluded, Tom took to the pulpit again.

"My friends. That was amazing. I do not remember the last time you sang so heartedly. I am sure we will be receiving a summons for noise ordinance violations. I will gladly pay it. Today, as you noticed, I am working a little off norm. As I prayed last night, the Lord did speak to me. He advised me of the direction that I needed to go today. Today, we are truly going to discuss the Lord's prayer.

"When the disciples were with Jesus, they asked him to teach them to pray. Not just the customary prayers required by Jewish tradition, but the prayers that Jesus himself prayed. That is when he taught them this prayer. Now mind you, man has put his own spin on the ending. There is no 'For thine is the kingdom, the power, and the glory forever' that was added for flare. Adds some to it, don't you think?"

The congregation laughed.

"Let's take a closer look at this prayer. The opening. Simple acknowledgment and reverence to God. 'Our Father who art in heaven. Hallowed be thy name.' That is like walking into the Oval Office and greeting the president, 'Mr. President, thank you for seeing me.' You are paying respect to God in his home, honoring his title and stature. All prayers should start with acknowledgment and reverence. He gave us life. He created the universe. He saved us. Simply letting him know that you recognize and respect that goes a long way. Think of it this way, who among us would walk into our grandparents' home and disrespect them by calling them by their names. My grandparents were Edith and Omar—don't laugh. They were great people. I would never even think about walking in their home or even asking them a question by first starting a sentence, 'Hey, Edith, can I ask your help. Or 'Yo, Omar1,' I do believe I would still be searching for my head if I had tried that."

The congregation laughed any louder. Martha reached up and tapped Jon on the shoulder and gave him a look of, we will talk about this later. He replied with a very respectful "Yes, ma'am" with eye contact.

"Next, we have 'your kingdom come, your will be done.' Now this is very important. His kingdom is coming. Are we ready? But more importantly, are we doing his will now? When we are in the lunchroom and the gossip begins, do we excuse ourselves? Do we put an end to it explaining that it is not right or do we join in? When we find a wallet in the park, do we look for the owner, or do we help ourselves first? When our brother or neighbor is hurting, do we turn a blind eye because the choices they made they deserve what they get, or do we come to their aid? When we have an argument with our spouse, do silence our tongue in our anger, or do we just let it rip because they started it? When someone makes a mistake, do we condemn them, or do we love them? I am not talking about loving what (they) did, but rather loving (them). When you are wronged by someone, do you forgive them and forget it, or do you forgive them and hold a grudge, or do you just not forgive and hold the grudge? How are we utilizing what we are learning in scripture and in studies to do his will here?

"My friends, let me explain a few things. I did solicit Jon to help me, but the challenges he brought up are real. He would not have known about them had I not told him. I am not lacking any material things. The church has provided a beautiful home, completely furnished and functional. I have food for my table. But I have since taken up a side hustle. At first it was just for fun, but then I found out I was gifted. I make leather belts. I sell them at random craft fairs. Please understand there is nothing sinful about having a side hustle that is legal. However, the reason behind the side hustle has become more clouded. At first it was a hobby. Then complement after complement. Then people were asking me to make them for them. I think you get the picture. After a while, it became a desire that took up much of my time and energy. Sometimes, too much. I logically deduced that it is a gift from God and should not squander it. Besides, I am just securing a small nest egg for when I retire. Right?"

The energy in the room was level. You could hear the wheels in everyone's head spinning. Some knew about the belts, some were astonished he could make belts, others were upset that he was making money, and they were paying him to pastor. Tim was locked in on every word that Tom was saying. An atomic bomb could have gone off, and Tim would not have budged. He felt like he was getting some answers that he did not even know that he wanted.

"'Give us this day our daily bread' is the next line. What exactly does this mean? For me, it means that I will ask God to provide all that I will need for the day's events. Money. Food. Resources. Knowledge. Wisdom. And most definitely love.

"When I pray this prayer, I say this line. I am asking God to provide all that I will need for the day's events. I am asking him to quell my innermost anxiety. I am asking him to give me the words to speak each time I encounter…anyone. I am asking him to provide for each and every insignificant detail of my day.

"Now here is the hard one. 'Forgive us our trespasses, as we forgive those who trespass against us.' We want to be forgiven, but we don't always forgive. Do you remember the story of the servant who was so far in debt that the master knew that he could never pay. The servant begged him to give him more time and the master had pity and forgave the debt. He now owed nothing. That was a wonderful thing that the master did, and you would think that the servant would be gracious beyond measure. But what did he do, he went and found someone who owed him just a tiny portion and when that person could not pay, he had the man incarcerated. Not very gracious, was he? When the master heard of this travesty, he immediately called for that servant, chastised him, and then sent him away to be tortured until (he) could pay (his) debt.

"Are we not like this servant in a lot of ways. You hurt me. I cannot forgive you. That is like saying it is okay what you did. My friends, this is the twist of the enemy. Forgiving someone, that does not give them a free pass. That simply says that you are not going to allow their transgressions to hinder your ticket to heaven. It is not going to steal your peace. It is not going to stop you from loving others…and loving them. After all, what have you done in your life, that you were forgiven for, by Jesus, that you really do not want anyone else to know? If he can forgive you and you essentially are a part of why he was on the cross in the first place, why can't you forgive someone here on Earth for whatever sin they caused against you? What are you gaining by holding on to their sin? The answer is nothing. As a matter of fact, you are marking an opportunity to lose everything. Remember, Jesus also said that if you hate in your heart, you have committed murder. No one here is a murderer, I hope.

"The last part of this prayer is 'Lead us not into temptation, but deliver us from the evil one.' This is really a no-brainer. Think about it. The Son of God…leading you 'to' temptation. Think about how ridiculous that is. It is not Jesus leading us to temptation, but the enemy. It is Jesus who needs to save us from the fowlers' snare.

"Too often, when things go wrong, we jump on board and start blaming God. God did not make you lust after that new secretary. God did not make you not correct the error at the restaurant. God did not cause you to lose your temper on the highway. God did not cause you join in that gossip at lunch. God died on the cross so that you would be saved from yourselves."

As he finished his sermon, Tom called for unbelievers to come forward to receive the gift of salvation. The congregation began to sing "The Old Rugged Cross," and Tim was moved. He had played on each and every word. He listened for the first time with his heart. He knew for a fact that this was the time for him to go forward and receive the gift of salvation through baptism. He was on the end of the row; he made his way down the aisle. No one was expecting him to go forward. Many had forgotten that he had not been baptized because he was so active in the church since the accident. Mary turned around and looked at Martha with astonished surprise. Martha was full of tears streaming down her face. Her prayers were answered; Tim was saved.

Chapter Twenty

Sitting at the breakfast table, Tim and Mary were enjoying their morning coffee and the beautiful sunrise. Tim had finished his first cup when he inquired, "Mary, what does it mean to be saved?" Taken back by his question, she sat her cup down and responded, "Do you mean saved by Jesus" With full question in his eyes, Mary could see that this was concerning question for Tim. How was she to answer this so that he understood its beauty. Mary took a minute to ask God to reveal to her the best way to explain this question's answer. Tim could see that she was formulating her answer and figured that she was talking to God about it also.

To give her a minute to process, he rose and fetched himself another cup of coffee. As he sat down again, his attention was pulled to the patio. There on the banister was an eagle. Seemed to be a young one, but an eagle no less. He had seen them in the meadow, but not this close to the house. Before he could get Mary's attention, the bird flew away. This interaction just made him even more con-fused. He had heard that animals could symbols or representations of God's message(s), and he figured that the squirrel analogy was like that, but what would an eagle have to do with his question to Mary?

"Tim," Mary began, "it is when we make the conscious choice to surrender ourselves to Jesus. To follow his teachings. To adhere to God's law. When we decide that we are going to put God first in everything…even family. Being saved is when we decided to take the narrow path, the difficult path, sometimes here on Earth, to make sure that we spend eternity in heaven with Jesus. Tim, there really is a hell. It really is fire, brimstone, and burning sulfur. It is as real as this coffee in my cup. *We* all have to make a choice on where we want to spend eternity. We do that by choosing a path."

"Didn't I do that when I woke up from the coma?" Tim asked genuinely.

"You took the first steps. You started attending church regularly. You started learning and asking questions. I have seen you make different, more godlike choices, but to say that you have surrendered… no, you haven't. Being involved in the church and fellowship, praying, studying, asking questions, all Christian traits, but that does not mean that you have surrendered to him. Think of this way: If you spend all your time in your shop, are you a hammer or a saw? Of course not. Doing all the Christian-like things does not make you a Christian. You have to surrender to him. That means that you have to give him your life, be reborn and transformed into a new creation in him."

Afraid that she may have gone too deep for Tim, she inquired, "Why are you asking about being saved? Are you scared?"

Tim sat silently sipping his coffee and then responded, "I had a dream last night. I dreamt that the service was God talking to Tom. During service. At the end of the sermon, I was compelled to go forward, and everyone was happy that I was saved. But I still do not understand how that works. How can I do all these things that I have done with the church, with Colton, with Paul…and not be saved? Am I not doing God's work?"

Mary sat there for moment and then asked, "Colton is Alex's father…right?"

Tim looked at her as though she had six eyes. "Yes?"

"So why didn't Alex run right up to him at Martha's and give him a great big hug and proclaim his love for his daddy?"

Still looking like she had six eyes, Tim replied, "Because he does not know Colton. Colton is a stranger to him."

Mary continued, "Exactly. Alex is not going to just let anyone in his inner most circle just because he says he is his dad. There is going to have to be some kind of proof. Just because you are 'doing' Christian things, God is not going to let you in his house, he does not know you. He wants to. He is proud of all that you have done, but he wants all of you. He wants proof in a sense that you are his son." There was slight silence in the room when Mary continued, "Tim, what are you scared of? What are you waiting for?"

"Did you see the eagle on the banister just a few minutes ago?" Tim asked.

"I did not. Why?" Mary replied. "Eagles have been playing in the meadow for a while. They are quite amusing to watch. There are a couple of younger ones flying around. They seem to be siblings because it looks as though they are annoying the other. Either that, or they are in love. I don't know which. But anyway, one of them sat on the banister after I asked you what it meant to be saved. Since seeing them in the meadow, I did a little research about them and their characteristics. Don't want to get near their talons. That would be another trip to the hospital. However, did you know that eagles are a sign of strength, courage, and wisdom? They are also associated with spiritual growth. Do you think God is telling me that it is time for me to make my commitment him?"

Mary sat in awe of Tim's account of the eagle and the information that he had learned. It also went along with the scripture that had come to mind at the beginning of this conversation, but she had dismissed as not making any sense at the time (Isaiah 40:31). Now it was all starting to make sense. "Yes, Tim, I believe that God is talking to you directly. He gave you the dream, and now he gave you a confirmation sign. It is time for you commit to him."

"Good morning, you serious-looking people, how are you doing this morning?" Colton appeared from the hallway still stretching and scratching his head. He headed over to the coffee pot and retrieved his cup for the morning. As he sat down at the table, Tim and Mary shifted their attention to Colton.

"How did you sleep?" Tim inquired.

"Ahhh, this is what I needed. This coffee is wonderful. I slept okay, but I sure do not know what I would do if you two didn't drink coffee. I feel like I wrestled a bear," Colton replied. "What are you two so serious about this morning?" he continued. They all sat there for a moment, and when Colton realized that the topic was not for him, he offered an ice breaker, "Can I ask you a different question?

I had a weird dream last night. I cannot make any sense of it. If I tell you, will you tell me what you think. Even if it sounds weird, please tell me." With a smirk of confidence returning to his face, Tim assured Colton that he would sure be able to tell him if he was weird. Mary gave Tim the "behave" look and assured Colton that they would do their best.

"It is kind of weird. Kind of jumbled too. None of it makes sense to me. The good thing is that there were no earie voices, but there were some earie images." He took another drink of coffee and reached for a pastry that was on the table. "This is good too. I don't care if it is a day old. Anyway, I was sitting in the bushes behind the church, like when Lucas found me that day. I was out of sight but had a full view of the picnic area and building. You both were there and Alex and Kim." He paused for another bite of the pastry. "Why am I so hungry?" he said with a mouthful. Tim and Mary just shook their heads and shrugged their shoulders. Colton continued, "I was hiding it seemed. You four were heading into the church. Behind the church appeared like a crimson backdrop—very, very red. Almost evil red, you see in the movies. There were shadows in the background. Then with a blink of an eye, there was an aged eagle so majestic that soared through the red, and it all turned white as snow. Then I woke up. What on Earth does that mean?" Colton grabbed the last pastry and continued to eat.

Tim and Mary looked at each other in complete astonishment. Colton had not been part of the conversation. He had not been anywhere near them as they spoke. How, unless it was God, did he know what Tim had dreamed. Tim excused himself to go shower and get ready for church. Mary explained that she was not sure what the dream meant, but perhaps it would be revealed at church today. Colton accepted her answer and stepped out on the porch for a breath of morning air. He was trying to reconcile in his mind how to best reach Alex, not lose Kim again and not lose all the ground he had gained in his mental health. He was scared but had a feeling that things were going to be worked out. As he stood in the morning gentleness, he prayed for God to show him what he was supposed to do. His prayers up to this point were superficial, but this one felt more earnest.

"God, I know you are speaking to me. I know it is you. I am committed to you. I do surrender to you. I don't know exactly how that works, but when you give me the nudge, I will do you what you ask of me." Tim prayed in the shower as the hot water flowed gingerly over him.

"Lord God, my Father. I can sense your presence in our house this morning. The signs are here. I pray Lord that Tim will commit to you today. That he will go forward and surrender to you completely. He is a good man, Lord. He is a faithful servant. I pray that he will show you today that he is your son." Mary prayed as she finished her coffee.

Chapter Twenty-One

As the three of them entered the church, a familiar song was playing in through the intercom, singing praises to God while going through the storms of life. You could see different people periodically singing along. The atmosphere was light and surreal at the same time. Mary could not put her finger on it but was convinced it had something to do with her conversation this morning with Tim.

"Good morning, Mary," Martha said as she entered the foyer. "Good morning, Mom. How was your breakfast table this morning?" Mary said. With an inquisitive look on her face, Martha asked how she knew that they had had an interesting breakfast conversation. The two ladies talked briefly and then made their way into the sanctuary.

"Good morning to everyone this morning. Welcome to our church. If you are new here, please sign our visitor book in the lobby. Also, if you are so inclined, leave an address and/or phone number if you would like further contact from one of our staff. We would like to also invite you all to stay after the serviced today for fellowship in the hall next door. We were going to have it outside, but the weather seems a bit off today, so we will have it next door. I do see that we have a few new faces. Welcome. As we begin our service this morning, I would like to start off with this song that tells us that we are not home yet, and that this is not where we belong." At this cue, the music began, and the congregation watched the view screen for the lyrics. As everyone sang, Tim fell into somewhat of a trance to the beat of the music and the message in the lyrics.

"Praise be to Jesus. He is our redeemer. Shall we sing of his greatness. Please turn to your hymnals or view on the screen, 'At the Cross.'" The leader sang loud and proud as the music echoed with the melody of angels throughout the rafters. Tim remained in a trance to the melody and lyrics. Mary had explained a shortened version of their breakfast conversation to Martha prior to them entering the sanctuary and when she noticed Tim's expression, she felt an overwhelming presence of the Lord in the church. He was definitely covering Tim. Mary began to weep. She knew what was happening and that her prayers were being answered. She nudged Martha, but she had already been alerted by the Holy Spirit that her son's life was being redeemed today.

"You all may be seated. Welcome to our church. God is in the house today." Shouts of "AMEN!" came in abundance. There was a new and refreshed state of awe in the sanctuary today. "Today, I will try to keep it in the 'allotted' time, but I make no promises," Tom began. "Today I am really feeling the Holy Spirit. He is so present here today. I have chills he is so present.

"Imagine if you will, you have purchased a home for you and your family. Life is good. The house is lovely. Over time, it gets some wear and tear, but it is still home. You fall on hard times and then fall behind in the mortgage. Your family has built memories here. You don't want to lose it to the bank. Due to the age and repairs needed, you cannot sell it to get out from under the mortgage. No one wants it. The bank representative comes to your home and says that you have thirty days to depart the property. You are too far behind, and the bank is no longer willing to work with you to get caught up. They are losing money on you and would rather sell it at auction to recoup some of their losses than to allow you to continue. The representative is cruel and unyielding. Cold and callous with each of their words. It was almost as though they were enjoying the sight of you becoming homeless and desperate.

"While you are pleading your case to the banker, a stranger appears out of nowhere. He listens to the banker and to you. The banker stops for a moment, turns to the gentleman, and tells him to get lost, that this is of no concern to him. Patiently, the stranger allows the banker to speak until he has completed all of his derogatory comments. Once the banker has finished, the stranger pushes through the banker to you, hands you the deed to your home, tells you that your bill has been paid in full. The stranger explains that your debt is paid, that he paid it for you because he loves you even though he has never met you. You open the paper and see across the deed PAID IN FULL.

"The banker, now extremely furious, grabs the deed to see for himself. He looks at the stranger and tells him that he is meddling in affairs that he need not be meddling in. The stranger simply tells the banker to be gone, that his business at this home is finished. Having no more authority at this residence, the banker scurries off. You look at the stranger and explain that you can never repay him. The stranger tells you that he knows that, but he would ask one thing. If you would dare to take up his challenge. Wondering what on Earth you could offer a person with such a means, you ask what it is that you could possibly give him that would repay the amount of debt he has paid for you. He simply says that he has a place for you in his company. That your talents are just what he is looking for. However, he leaves the choice up to you.

"Now, one might be inclined to take the money and run as it were, but what happens when that next shiny object comes along? Will you mortgage your home again, or will you be able to withstand the pressures and walk away. Almost all of us love a good shiny something. Those who are truly intrigued as to what makes a guy like this tick, they want to know his secrets to success. They want to be like him. He is offering a job to someone he does not even know with a salary to cover all your debts. Both are tempting. Which one would you choose?"

Tim's eyes were fixed on Tom. He could not turn his head or hardly blink his eyes. He was so engrossed in what Tom was saying. *Was this what Mary was talking about?* such thoughts paraded through his mind like a carousel.

"In this story, the banker is the enemy. He only wants what is his. If he can make you miserable in the process and steal your peace and joy, all the better. Once he has those, he can dangle a carrot in front of you and grab your soul. The stranger, you guessed it, is Jesus. He has paid your debt of sin in its entirety. When they nailed him to the cross, your debt was paid. All he is asking is that you join his company. Will you faithfully and freely join his company? Serve him and follow his rules? Will you go places that no one wants to go to tell others about the Good News? Will you walk the narrow pathways, seeking out the good soil to plant seeds of love and fellowship? Jesus wants you. He wants your talents. He wants your passion. He wants your commitment. He wants your love.

"Are you willing to give yourself, your talent, your love, your faith, your commitment above all else to him? To the man who came to earth, died a horrible death then rose again so that you may live for eternity in paradise."

As Tom was speaking, Tim was listening, there was a change in the lighting from the windows. A slight crimson hue fell across the sky. Colton looked at Mary with fear in his eyes. It was from his dream. Alex tapped Colton on the shoulder to show him the pair of eagles sitting in the windowsill. Colton jerked around to Mary who was lost in the moment. Tim was still fixated on Tom.

"If there be anyone here today that has not given their life to Jesus, completely and earnestly, I plead with you to search your hearts and consider joining the company of the Man who has paid your debt."

As Tom finished that sentence. He had barely uttered the last word. Tim stood up from his seat. Made his way to the aisle and began his way to Tom. At that moment, the pair of eagles ascended upward, and the crimson hue was gone. Tim approached Tom and told him that he wanted to serve…that he wanted to give all of his life to Jesus. He now understands what that means. He wanted God first in his life. Tom asked a series of questions that Tim proudly and adamantly answered with his devotion to God. Tom asked him if he was ready for the outward gesture of baptism, and Tim explained that he was. When Tim was brought up out of the water, the ray of sunlight that penetrated the windows was blinding.

The congregation began singing "Now I Belong to Jesus." Praises and accolades were shouted as the lost sheep had been found.

The angels rejoiced and Martha wept uncontrollably. Her prayers had been answered. Her boys were home, and her son was now saved. Her life was now complete.

With tears from her eyes streaming down her face, Mary turned to Colton. "Do you understand what is going on? Tim gave his life to serve God. He has been redeemed. I could tell you stories of things that he has done that were not even in the category of even partially nice…they were downright wrong. But none of that matters. Jesus has washed all his sins away, and he is now a new man. His past does not matter. What he did before does not matter. The only thing that matters now is how he serves his God. Colton, that could be you. What has happened in your past does not matter. Whatever sins you have committed do not matter. You will be a new man…if you surrender to Jesus."

Colton looked at Kim and Alex. Then he looked at Mary. He had just watched his mentor, whom he thought already was Christian make it publicly known that he was surrendering everything. Mary insisted that freedom was within Colton's grasp. He just needed to reach out and take hold of the Master's hand.

"You are too far gone. Don't be fooled. That could never be you. You killed your buddies. You have killed innocent people. You will never be good enough for Jesus. You left your family for nearly twenty years. You disowned your son. You will never—"

The ugliness running through his head was too much. Colton screamed, "ENOUGH!"

The church fell silent. Alex looked out the window and told Kim that the red tint was back in the sky. Kim looked at Mary and then to Paul and then to Colton. Colton was sitting there with his hands over his head, trembling. Imagery of the war-torn thoughts blowing up his mind. The idea of the squirrel being brave. Talks that he and Tim have had over colas in the shop. The love that has been shown to him in this town. The reintroduction to his true love. The introduction to his son. The friendships and bonds that he has made since being home. The peace that he had encountered, drowning out the voices. Tim, soaked to the bone, dripping water through the church, made his way to Colton. No one said a word.

"Colton," Tim started softly, "Colton, my brother. The turmoil that you are feeling is normal. The enemy is after you. He sees you are on the precipice to cross the great chasm to the Father. He is going to jump all over this quickly. He almost had you and we intervened. Come with me. Come with me and dedicate your life. Give your soul to Jesus. I am probably the most hard-headed person in his room next to my mother and brother. I get it now. I thought I was doing enough by coming to church, but...I will tell you. I always knew that there was something missing. It is not missing anymore. I can feel the power of the Holy Spirit running through me. I feel like I would truly wrestle a bear and win now. Come with me. Give yourself to him."

"*You are worthless...*" As the voice began to speak, Tim renounced him in the name of Jesus and sent him packing. Colton raised his head and looked into Tim's eyes. The reflection of two soaring eagles was there. Colton rose from his seat and followed Tim to the altar. Tom had made his way back to the front. He asked Colton a series of questions to which he answered in sobs of sorrow for all he had done. Tom asked him if he was ready to make the outward gesture of obedience in the form of baptism, Colton cried that he did. When he came up out of the water, the red hue from the sky was gone, the eagles were soaring above the church, and the light that penetrated the church windows was twice as bright as before.

Chapter Twenty-Two

Puddles of water were throughout the sanctuary from Tim traipsing back to Colton and leading him back to the altar. Piles of tissues were all over the floors and pews from tears of joy and awe. Murmurs of what just took place were all about the sanctuary, about what they all had just witnessed. A shadow lingered in the far back. It appeared to be cornered and blocked in, almost caged.

One small boy had been very observant during the service. This had been the best one ever in his mind. It was exciting. He had questions but was unsure of whom to ask. As he processed everything that he had seen, he decided that his mom and dad were right: Go to the source. For him, that was Tim. He decided that when he got the chance and he could get to him because grown-ups were everywhere, he would ask him.

Martha and Mary embraced with tears of joy and adulation for what they just witnessed. Martha aske Mary if she knew and Mary explained the conversation that they had over coffee, but that they had conversation like this before and nothing but a normal service attending. Mary explained that she was in just as much pleasurable shock as everyone else. "Could you hear Tim when he was talking to Colton?" Martha asked.

"No, it was like he was whispering. And then for whatever reason, he shouted. I don't understand. I figured I would ask him about it later," Mary replied.

"Mom," Alex began, "what just happened?" Kim looked at her son and explained that his father just took the first step to putting his demons to bed forever. Confused, Alex asked, "What do you mean?"

"Alex, Cole just surrendered his life to Christ like you did back home. It was a bit more dramatic, but he is facing some serious internal demons, and he felt like he did not deserve God's grace and forgiveness. I am not sure what Tim said to him, or why he yelled, but it worked. He is one of God's family now, just like you and me." Alex, still a little confused but starting to understand, hugged his mom tightly.

Paul, who had sat next to Martha, wrapped his arms around his mom and told her that he did not know that Tim had never stepped forward. He thought that after he woke up from the coma that he had made that decision. Martha explained that Tim did begin attending church and working in the ministries, but he never surrendered. It was not his time…until today.

Tim and Colton were in the back changing clothes and drying off when Colton asked Tim how many languages he spoke. Tim looked at him funny and replied, "Two, English and hillbilly…oh, wait…three…sarcasm is my specialty. Why do you ask?"

"Seriously, Tim…do you speak another language because when you came down to me, what you were speaking was not English. It was like an Arabic syntax. I recognized it from my deployments, but I could not understand you. Not the words anyway. Then when you yelled, it was when the voices started up again…but they barely got started when you yelled." Tim finished getting dressed and looked at Colton with a sincere yet perplexed look.

Knock, knock.

"Are the two newest additions to the kingdom dressed?" Tom announced as he opened the door slightly.

"Ahhh," Tim screeched in a little girl tone. Tom opened the door the rest of the way and entered the room. "Gentlemen"—shaking his head in astonishment and adoration—"gentlemen, my brothers. You two never cease to amaze me. Tim…I thought I had convinced you many times before, but you never came forward. Colton, my dear new friend. This is the first step in conquering those demons."

Tim and Colton, without any warning, tackled Tom and said in unison, "Love you, Daddy." The three men lay giggling when Mary knocked and cracked the door. When she saw the men laughing on the floor, she just quietly closed the door and stood guard as the children finished their romper room activities. She had never seen such commotion after a baptism, but seeing how it was Tim *and* Colton, it did not surprise her at all.

When the wrestling match concluded, and all three men caught their breath, Tom looked at Tim and said, "Tim, I need to know… okay, I don't need to know. I would like to know, what made you choose today? Why did you choose today to come forward? You and I have spoken many times about this, and each time I thought you would commit. The next Sunday would appear."

"Pastor, I have come so close…so many times. But for whatever reason, I just couldn't make myself. Something always told me to wait," Tim began. "This time, I don't know…it was different. Maybe it is because of the dream I had…but I think it was more of the forgiveness I saw when Kim…" Tim stopped and turned to Colton. "The open forgiveness that Kim gave to Colton on Martha's front walk. After that night and the breakfast, the time with Paul talking about brother stuff and Carson, realizing how blessed I am to be here and that I have my own family…intact. Tom, I should not be here, you know that. That drunk driver should have gotten my life, but the prayers over me while I was in the coma, Momma's constant prayers over me since I was kid, all of it. I finally 'heard' Him. Not only heard, but finally obeyed."

Colton listened intently to Tim as he explained to Pastor Tom his decision. As Tim concluded his comments, Colton looked at him and asked, "Why me?" Tim looked at Colton with all sincerity and love, "My brother, from the day I met you trying to burn my property down—just kidding—I knew there was something about you. When I got back to the house and confirmed to Mary that she saw your flame—how, I have *no* idea—and her restlessness that night. I knew there was something about you. God kept leading me to friend you. A lot inside me told me to protect Mary, but I could tell that there was no need for protection. The odds of meeting Kim and Alex and them being a part of you…there is no other answer but God. Even I know that. I am pretty dumb when it comes to this God stuff, but even an old dog like me knows that was totally God."

Colton and Tom listened to Tim's testimony to Colton. Then Tom asked Colton, "What did Tim say to you to make you come forward?" Colton looked at Tom, hesitated to answer, but then said, "I could not understand him, he was speaking in an Arabic language of sorts, at least that is what I think it was. It sounded a lot like how the older natives spoke when I was deployed. I could 'feel' his words. I could not understand them. I could understand him without understanding if that makes any sense. Then he yelled and I felt freedom. I didn't want that to end. So I went forward as fast as could. I felt like freedom was up there in surrender. I have not felt this free in a very long time."

Tim was still confused as to what Colton was talking about because he felt as though he was speaking English the whole time. Tom had a good idea but did not want to cause any more confusion to Tim.

Tim, Colton, and Tom emerged from the room to a hall full of praise parishioners. As everyone came up to welcome them both to the family to give hugs and offer assistance in their growth. A young boy came up and tugged at Tim's shirt tail.

"Excuse me, sir" came a small soft voice. Tim looked down to see the eyes of a very determined young man.

"Yes, sir, may I help you." Tim dropped down to one knee to look the young man in the eye.

The young boy looked Tim square in the eyes and said, "Why did you yell those funny words in church?"

With the same bewilderment, Tim looked up at Tom who did not have answer. Colton had already told him what he heard…sort of…Tim had no answer for this young man. "I don't know what—"

Before he could continue, an older gentleman who was quite educated came forward and asked the young man if he heard this: "Ezev…mat adonai." With eyes of excitement, the young boy said, "Yes, that was it." Tim, now really confused, looked at the older man. Tom was now very interested in what was transpiring. The group of people were just as intrigued as ever. They thought service was wild; it was still happening. *No* one had left the hall.

The older gentleman asked for a chair. He sat down and asked the young boy to climb on to his lap. He began to explain that he was sitting near Tim and Colton. He could hear everything that was going on. Though his hearing is not what it used to be, today God blessed him with perfect hearing so that he could explain what happened. "You see, young sir, Satan has been after all of us for a very long time. He wants our souls in hell with him. He does not like Jesus, but you knew that already, didn't you?"

The boy nodded. "I know this man here"—he pointed to Tim—"for a very long time. I have known his momma even longer. I know that she has been praying very hard for him to meet Jesus in a good way. Today, he did that. As Pastor Tom was teaching his lesson, God told me to start praying. He didn't tell me why, he just told me to start praying. So I did. When I saw Tim go forward, God told me to pray harder that the devil was in our church and trying to take someone away. I continued pray. God blessed us with beautiful brightness when Tim came up from the water. But just as he did, I could feel cold darkness near me. I prayed even harder. Then I could hear Tim talking to his friend. He was speaking in ancient Arabic. Not sure why God chose that language or why he gave me the chance to hear and understand it, but it is a beautiful language. Tim was explaining to his friend that it was his time too and to get rid of the voices that he needed to surrender to Jesus. When the devil thought that he was losing…and he was…he started speaking to Tim's friend again. That is when you heard the funny words. That is Hebrew for 'be gone by God,' probably not a 'direct and correct' translation but very close. Because Tim was now a child of God, he could command the devil away and the devil had to obey him."

The little boy and all in the hall listened with such intensity that you could hear each breath individually. After a bit of silence at the end of his explanation, he reached out to Tim and said, "God be with you, my son. Your dad would have been so proud of you today. I know your momma is."

"Thank you, sir," Tim replied.

Colton reached over and grabbed Tim in a massive bear hug, crying heavily sobs of love and release. Mary and Martha joined on one side of the two men, Kim and Alex and Paul on the other. In the background, someone started singing "Amazing Grace." Before it concluded, there was not a dry eye in the house, and the shadow was still pinned in the corner.

Chapter Twenty-Three

Martha insisted that everyone come to her house for lunch. Tim, Mary, and all the kids. Paul, Colton, Kim, and Alex. She explained that it would just be sandwiches, but she needed to talk to them all. She had something to share and now was the perfect time to do so.

Mary and Kim helped Martha retrieve all the necessities for lunch. She even insisted that they use the fine china from the pantry. She really despised paper plates but decided to go out of her comfort zone today. Mary nearly choked on laughter when Martha called it fine china. Kim giggled because that was her fine china.

Once everyone was seated at the table, Martha told them all to fix themselves a plate, that she would be back to the table in a few minutes. As she was about to leave, she stopped and told everyone to wait, bowing her head she began to pray, "Dear Lord," and instantly, everyone bowed their heads, "Dear Lord, you have heard this woman's prayers and pleas. I thank you, dear Lord, and ask that you bless this meal that you have prepared for all of us. In Jesus's name, amen." The table articulated in unison, "Amen." Martha left the room, and they began to fix their plates. Small talk about today's events consumed the conversation. Just as the conversation was bustling good with questions and comments, Tim and Paul looked at each other and instinctively excused themselves from the table. Mary looked curiously at Jon, but both remained seated.

Tim and Paul entered the hallway leading to Martha's room. Just as they were about to announce themselves and offer help, they heard Martha. She was speaking but in a broken and weeping voice. Tim went to find out what was wrong when Paul stopped him, placed his finger over his lips and motioned for them to listen.

"Father, oh, my Father. You have heard my pleas. Please forgive me for not having faith. For not believing you had heard my cries. Father, oh, my Father. You are the all-powerful and oh so merciful. You have blessed me in more ways than I can count. You know the hairs on my head to the feelings of my heart. You know the cells from within me to the existence of my being. *You*, oh Lord, have made my family whole. *You*, oh Lord, have saved an old woman's family from hell. I am not worthy of your mercies, yet you graced me with my answered prayers. I know, Lord, this is not a fancy and wordy prayer, but it is pure."

The boys silently crept down the hallway to Martha's room and found her on her knees bowed in submission in prayer. Martha cried out to God in thanksgiving, siting that he had saved her boys from certain death. That he had empowered her with certain understanding. That he had gifted her with certain gifts. That she was eternally grateful. As she concluded her prayer, Tim and Paul stepped silently backward as to not be seen. Wiping tears from their eyes from what they had heard, they quietly returned to the table. Mary and Kim looked at the men and could see a difference in their demeanor.

Soon after they returned to the table, Martha called to from the hallway for Jon to meet her at her bedroom door. Obediently, he went to his grandmother. "Jon, I need you to take this trunk to the dining room for me please."

He replied, "Yes, ma'am." Jon grabbed ahold of the trunk handles and lifted it to carry. It was moderately heavy, but he was not about to let his grandma down nor was he about to let Todd think he could not do it on his own. Brotherly rivalry, ya know.

Jon brought the trunk into the dining room and set it down on a stand where Martha directed. Standing by until released, Jon shot Todd a glimpse of "I'm the favorite and don't forget it" smirk. Todd just rolled his eyes with a "whatever" look. Mary caught both looks and smiled. Martha told Jon to have a seat and to make himself a sandwich. She then began to fidget with the lock on the trunk. Once it opened, a whiff of her husband came out in force. The trunk had been sealed for several years…on purpose. Emotions overcame Martha, Tim went to get up, but she waved him off. She worked through the tears and love then turned to her family.

"Boys," she began, "I know you heard my prayers. It's okay. I am not mad. I am so—" She stopped for a moment. "I am so proud of both of you. You were supposed to hear, God summoned you to my room. It was so that you knew firsthand. So that you knew that I never gave up on you. That you heard it from me…to God…so that you knew without a doubt that I love you more than imaginable." She then turned her eyes to Jon, Todd, Margret, and Janey. "You kids…are a perfect reflection of your parents. You have had some rocky points, some high points, some okay points, but you are all faithful to the One who knows you best. It shows in your everyday life." Catching her composure, she turned to Colton. "Young man. I have known you for almost all your life. See, I knew your father before you ever moved here." The table became even more silent than before. No one knew this. Colton sat in quiet wonder. "Butch used to be a righteous man. But he was changed in the war. He would not talk about it, and he ended up taking it out on you and your mom. He told your mom that you ran away, not that he threw you out. She was heartbroken. It wasn't long after that she left him. No one knew where she went. Rumors came that he had killed her, but that is not true. I do not know what you heard, but I can tell you where she is if you want to see her. I have kept in touch over the years."

Floods of tears fell from Colton's face. He had always wondered why she had never reached out to him and why his letters were returned to sender. Kim reached out to him and held him close.

"Sarah lives in a small town in Montana. No one there really knows her. She became a recluse, and most think that she is crazy. She doesn't care. She lost you. Then lost her love, Butch, to war. She kept in touch with me because I was the only one who would not judge her. I have not told her that you were here. I have not done that because there were other battles you were fighting and that would have just added fuel to the enemy's fire. *You* have defeated the enemy today. It is safe for you to know. We will discuss exact locations later."

Tiny let out a little wail; Janey removed herself from the table to tend to her son. Maggie followed her mom. Once Janey returned to the table, Martha continued.

"Alex, my dear Alex. You are in a difficult situation. You are new believer, still full of a lot of the world. Satan is after you, son. You have to stay strong in the faith. Send him packing every time when doubt enters your mind. He came after you when you first came here. He came after you in the church. He came after you when you all went to the park. Stand firm, young man. I know that God has a mighty plan for you. You are a warrior…the warrior God has chosen to fight a battle for him. Do not lose hope. You are a child of God."

Martha then turned her attention to the trunk. A picture of her late husband, Phil, was gently placed on top. Beneath were a few of his favorite clothes and a few items he held close to his heart.

"Tim, Paul, your dad was a faithful man. *No*, he did not attend church the way we do. He did his praying in the woods. He worshiped in private. I tried and tried to get him to come with us, but he felt closer to God on the creek bank or leaning up against a tree. The day before he died, he showed me these." Martha reached down into the bottom of the trunk and pulled out two very used Bibles. One had belonged to his father and the other to his mother. Inside each Bible was letter to his sons but were only to be given to them when they could fully comprehend the love in them. Martha handed the boys each a Bible. Each letter within the Bible was specifically addressed to Paul and to Tim. The letters were specifically written to each of them from their father. As they began to read the heartfelt love emanating from the pages, Martha turned to the younger generation. "Jon, Margaret, Todd, Janey, your grandfather never really knew you, but he did." She reached into the trunk again and pulled out four brand-new Bibles, each with a specific letter enclosed for each of his grandchildren.

Martha had not told anyone about this trunk or the gifts that lie inside. She was held to a bond from Phil to not let them leave her sight until it was the right time. She held on to them until she felt Phil tell her to surrender the gifts. After today's events, she knew it was time.

"Boys, your dad's fall was an accident. We did not know at the time that he was suffering from a balance issue. The autopsy showed that he had a seizure, and it was likely generated by the other underlying issues that he never shared with anyone. Not even me. I had no idea the battles he was enduring. I did not tell you all this before because I felt it was easier to let the fall seem like an accident than your dad being weaker. Please forgive me."

Tim and Paul got up and embraced their mother tightly. Both expressed that forgiveness was not needed—that they loved her unconditionally and now really know how to do that. Real love.

Chapter Twenty-Four

Martha closed up the trunk then took her place at the end of the table. She looked over the family she was blessed with. She remembered the different trials that they had overcome. She looked directly at Tim, burst into tears, and once composed, she cried out, "Tim, my son. You have been a blessing and a torment. You have resisted all attempts to come to Jesus. I know that you blamed God for your dad's death. I know you had hardships that you could only see him as the meaning. When you failed to come to church that day, I asked God to bring you home. Whatever it took. I knew that your coma was his last chance to reach you. I knew that if you failed to hear him then, you would be condemned. I prayed so hard that that God would reach you inside your mind." Martha paused and reached for Tiny. Holding the young lad in her arms, tears poured from her eyes. Switching her focus and words to the baby, she said, "You, young man, saved your grandpa and didn't even know it. I cannot wait to watch you grow up with your grandpa teaching you all about life." Placing her finger on Tiny's little nose, she continued, "You are a definite gift from God. Please listen to your grandpa, and don't be afraid to ask him questions he will have to think about. It is good for him to have to think a little bit." A light chuckle commenced from the table.

While she was still holding the baby, Martha continued. She looked at Paul. "Paul, you and Melony are meant to be together. Carter's death was not your fault. There was nothing you or she could do. It was necessary for you to find your true calling. You had to feel that pain and that anguish. You had to feel that suffering to understand the suffering that Kim and Alex were going through. God used you as an angel of mercy on their lives." Martha turned her tears and focus to the newly formed family. "Alex, young man. You have a rough road in front of you. The enemy knows you are vulnerable. He is going to use your father's absence and your mom's struggles to hold a grudge between you and Colton. You will need Jesus to help you fight those urges to fight against Colton's appearance in your lives."

When Martha had stopped for a moment, Alex asked, "Ma'am, I have a question. If you do not mind." Pleased, Martha told him to please ask. Alex looked at her. "How do you know all this? I am not trying to be smart, but I do not understand how you know all this. I know that older people, not that you are old…" His attempt to retract the statement brought a quick giggle from everyone and a smile from Martha.

"Alex I am older, yes, you are correct."

Sighing a relief, Alex continued, "I guess I just don't understand how you know that all you know is from God."

Martha handed Tiny to Jack and looked at Alex with warmth in her eyes. "Alex, I could spend hours talking about this, but the true and simple answer is 'faith.' I know that seems skimpy in an answer, but it is truly the answer. I have been praying for years for Tim to let go of his anger. I have prayed for peace for Paul. I guess in a way, I even prayed for you without even knowing it. See, young man, your entrance into our lives has turned the corner on my son's lives. Everything happens for a reason. We do not always know the reason, but in the end of that journey, the reason comes clear."

Alex accepted her response and sat silently for a while. The others spoke of the day's events and Martha's giving, then Alex said, "Excuse me please. Can I ask one more question?" Everyone turned their attention to him, and Martha said to proceed. Alex looked at Martha and asked, "Ms. Martha, may I call you grandma too?"

Martha stood up and went over to Alex, grabbing him up into a grandma-type hug. "Yes, sir, you sure may."

After lunch, Alex asked Paul and Colton if they could have a man to man talk. Colton looked at Kim. She shrugged and said that he would love to. Paul, Colton, and Alex walked out to the back patio.

Paul looked at Alex and said, "Yes, sir. What did I goof up now?" Trying to bring a little levity to the situation. Colton smiled and said, "I am sure it was me."

Alex looked at both of them with a determined look on his face. "You both are fathers to me. One biologically and one not. One was there when I was in a dark place, one not. I am really conflicted and confused. But I know that I need you both." He turned his attention to Colton, "I want to hit and stomp and tear you apart. I want to cuss you and tell you to stay away. To tell you about all the suffering you caused when you *lied*, but I can't." He turned to Paul. "I want to embrace you as my dad. Love you like you loved me. Tell you that I want you to be my dad." After a brief pause to compose himself, he whispered, "But I can't." Paul and Colton both reached to embrace Alex, but he pulled away. In a more commanding and defiant tone and posture, Alex looked at both of them. "I am a man now. Not legally maybe, but I have been the man of this family since the day I was born. I made a lot of mistakes. I hurt my mom a lot, but I never lied to her. Defied her…absolutely. Hurt her heart, yes, I did. Lie to her, never did. When I felt a lie coming, I just left in a fit of rage. The day I tried to rob you, Paul, was after an argument with Mom. I was going to show her that I didn't need anyone. But the truth is…I do need…I need her…and…I need both of you. Both of you have brought something to my life, and I cannot continue to grow as a man without you both." Tears were streaming down his face as he pronounced his love for both Colton and Paul and his need to have both of them in his life peacefully. Alex explained that he understood the complex nature of this scenario, but vehemently expressed his desire to have two dads in his life. Two dads who will love him. Two dads that will be there. Two dads that will hold him accountable. Since he had spent most of his life without a dad, he figured that God had given him two dads because he was such a handful.

By now, all three men were emotional wrecks. Colton and Paul both reached for Alex and this time when Alex pulled away the men grabbed his shirt and pulled him in. The embrace was so strong that Alex melted into their chests weeping. What he had been longing for and didn't even know it had been granted to him.

Colton whispered, "Son, I will never leave you again. I am so sorry. Please forgive me."

Paul whispered, "Son, you saved my life, I will love and stand by you always." Both older men held Alex and told him that they would agree to his terms of two dads.

From the window, Kim watched as her son let down his walls of protection of being let down or hurt. She watched her little boy weep as though the monsters were after him again. She watched her little boy become a man—a true man.

With tears of love and joy pouring down her cheeks, Kim looked at Martha and thanked her for her hospitality and for sharing some history with all of them. She further asked if she would be kind enough to let them stay a few more days. Kim was going to quit her job and move to town so that she and Colton could start fresh. She would start looking for work immediately. Martha expressed that she and Alex could stay as long as they needed to but to be cautious of making hasty decisions. This was a decision that they needed to make as a family. Martha continued, "I know where your heart is, but remember that the enemy is still lurking about. Do not give him an opening or an opportunity." With a kind smile of understanding, Kim let Martha know she would speak to Colton and Paul about her idea, and she reassured Martha that she would pray on it some more, but she was certain that this was the path God had set forth for her.

The evening drew to a close. Tim and Mary excused themselves and returned to their home. Jack and Janey took the two little ones home; they were getting restless without their toys. Paul went for a walk to meditate. Todd, Jon, and Margaret all left as well. Each giving appropriate hugs and love to Martha. Kim invited Colton and Alex to sit in the backyard and get acquainted…and to possibly speak of what is to come in the future. Martha cleaned up the dining room table and the kitchen. She retired to her sitting chair with her Bible in hand and began her evening devotion to God. The day had been filled with all sorts of emotions and revelations. The road ahead would be an adventure for sure; however, right now, she needed one man. She needed God, so she climbed up on his lap, laid her head on his chest, and began to talk to her Father.

Chapter Twenty-Five

Kim took Martha's advice. Seeing the wisdom she portrayed at lunch, Kim knew that Martha was a true woman of God.

After everyone had left for the evening, Alex had retired to his room to watch videos on his phone. Paul said that he needed to pack because he had booked a midmorning flight back home. He was overwhelmed with exuberance from the church service, the lunch exposé, the true and complete honesty from Alex, and a new desire to return to his home and sit down with Meloney. He really needed to apologize and talk to her. There was a lot of unresolved territory they needed to mend, and he felt as though it was time. Kim retired to her own room, closed the door, turned off all the lights, sat in the corner reading chair by the window and began to pray.

Meanwhile, Tim, Mary, and Colton had returned home. The ride was silent. Tim had asked Mary to drive; he said that he could not focus on the road. Today's activities had exhausted him beyond exhaustion. As they pulled into the drive, Colton excused himself and went to his room. Tim and Mary retired to the kitchen table with a cup of coffee. It was later than they normally had coffee, but they both needed something warm and soothing. They opted for the less potent decaf since bedtime was not far off. Sitting at the table, they made small talk but mostly sat in silence and processed the events of the day.

Colton lay in his bed staring at the ceiling. He replayed each of the events in order. Starting with the topic of the service, to Tim going forward, the tugging going on inside of him. Massive fear, confusion, anger, hatred, love, confusion, hatred, love, warmth, love, peace, bold colors of red and black…blood, body parts, it should have been him; his mind was racing. He had to get out of the church, then Tim spoke to him in Arabic and he understood him…kind of. The massive wave of emotions that had flooded him in the church, but all were stilled when he went forward and submitted his life. He did not understand. Then the old man who explained everything, followed by the revelations to the family by Martha. Add to that Alex's confession. Him and Paul coming together as two dads with one son to mentor and advise and hold true. All this in one big melting pot, now Colton had to make a decision, stay here, and ask Kim to stay; go to Martha and get Sarah's address; go back with Kim and Alex and find work—what was he going to do? What was he supposed to do? As the multitude of thoughts, ideas, fears, and possibilities flooded through Colton's mind, he prayed silently…reverently… asking the Holy Spirit to please guide him.

When morning came, no one was moving all that fast. The emotions of yesterday had taken three days' worth of energy out of everyone. Colton excused himself after breakfast coffee and explained that he needed to go to the brook and talk to the squirrel and chipmunk. Mary and Tim laughed but knew that he was closest to God when he was outside.

"Mary," Tim began, "I need to tell you something."

Mary turned to face Tim and offer her full attention. The tone in his voice was a cross from their wedding vows and when he came home from the hospital. She knew whatever he had to say was extremely important.

"Mary, you are my one true love. I have known that from the first day I saw you. I knew you were going to be my wife. Even after we had that big blow up, I knew you would say yes when I proposed. You produced four beautiful children. You raised four very different, very independent, very loving children. You did that. And you put up with me. When you were worried that I was lost forever, you prayed for God to do *whatever* it took to get my attention, and when he did, you never left my side. I do not know what I did to be blessed with a woman like you. I do not deserve you. You never pressed. You never preached. You only loved. No matter what I did, you loved. I want to give you what you have given me. I want us to be a power-house for God. Will you pray with me every day? Every night? Teach me and guide me to understand the stories? Will you forgive me for not being the man you needed me to be?" Tim's voice was breaking and pushed through to the end.

Mary sat sobbing in wonderous love for her husband. God had answered her prayers in abundance. She had only asked that he save him; now he has given her a warrior. As they hugged in the morning light, tears of everlasting love and radiance of God's love shrouded them like a full covering umbrella.

"You are wasting your time. They are not even home. That man who abandoned you isn't even inside. He left. He left you again. When will you learn that he is nothing but a loser," a chilling voice whispered in Kim's ears as she continued to ring the doorbell of Tim and Mary's. She had heard their voices inside, but they did not answer. Finally, she opened the door and witnessed their embrace. There was some-thing special about the vision of their love. Kim so wanted to have such love. She was willing to do whatever it took. She knew she and Colton were to be a family; now they had to figure out how. And that voice was like a fly buzzing in her ear; if she could have swatted it, she would have.

"Um…excuse me?" Kim said. Neither one heard her. A little louder, she repeated herself, "Um, excuse me…Mary…is Colton here?"

Tim and Mary looked at the door to see Kim standing there. Their faces covered in tears, flushed with emotions. Neither wanting to let go of the other. They explained that Colton had gone to the brook to talk to a squirrel and a chipmunk. That Kim just needed to follow the trail, that it would lead her straight to him. As she was about to close the door behind her, Tim belted out, "Be wary of the turds!" He and Mary started laughing. Kim grinned with confusion and continued on her way to find Colton.

She followed the path as they had instructed and found Colton sitting on the bridge. He appeared to be deep in thought. She did not want to interrupt, but she knew that she had to.

"Colton," she half whispered.

"He belongs to me. I don't care what he thinks he did yesterday. He is mine. He has been and I am not letting him go. Do you understand me!"

"GET BEHIND ME, SATAN!" Kim yelled at the top of her voice.

Colton jolted, "Kim?"

"Cole, I am so sorry. I did not mean to startle you. I need to talk to you. It is very important."

"Kim, I need to talk to you too."

The two looked deep into the other's eyes. Both wanting so desperately to tell their side, but fearful of the response.

"This will never work. This will never work. She is going to reject you because you are a LIAR. You will fail her like you did your squad."

A cool air brushed over Colton's neck and tensed up. "Are you all right, Cole?"

He replied, "I am fine, the voices caught me off guard, and it wanted to tell me I was a failure and a liar. I am, but I am not. If that makes any sense."

"It does. That is why I yelled. That same voice told me the same thing. I know you and you are not a liar. You are my Cole."

The two embraced. The warmth of their soles touching with each beat of their heart.

"Cole," Kim began, "Alex and I have to return home. I have used up all the time I can without jeopardizing my job. Right now, it is the only job I have, and it does nice by us." She paused for a minute and hushed him as he tried to speak. "I want you to be a part of our family. I want us to be a family. I love you. I always have. I have already forgiven you for choosing to not be a part of our lives before now. You had your reasons, and we can work through all that later. But right now, I want you to go to Montana. Find your mom. Mend fences, fill voids, and repair broken hearts. That is where you need to be right now. I have told Alex what I was going to tell you and he said that if you come to our home before you make it right with your mom, he will take you to the woodshed himself."

Tears flooded down his face. This was the conversation he was trying to figure out how to have with her. Because he had been absent and now they were together, he did not want her to think he was running away. "Kim, I never stopped loving you. I didn't love myself and knew that I could not be the husband you deserved. I am sorry you had to raise Alex on your own. You did a wonderful job. He has turned into a fantastic young man."

The two walked back up to the house and explained to Tim and Mary what they had discussed. Kim thanked them for bringing in Cole and taking such good care of him. She explained that she and Alex would be leaving in a couple of days on a flight back home. She had contacted her boss, and they were happy to have her coming back.

After Colton put Kim and Alex on the plane, he drove straight over to Martha's. The two of them had a long, long talk about Colton's dad, mom, and everything that had happened. Tears flowed plentifully, and Martha asked if he would like to call his mom. In disbelief, he said that he would.

Martha picked up her cell phone and called Sara. "Good afternoon, my friend. How are you doing this beautiful day?" Martha said in her normal loving voice.

"I am fine. It is too cold, and people won't leave me alone as usual. You don't ever call me, what's wrong?" Sara expressed concern that her friend was in some kind of trouble.

"Sara, you are such a worrywart. If I can figure this out, will you switch to a video call? I miss your face."

"Good grief, woman. Hang on a minute."

Martha turned the phone away for a second and whispered in Colton's ear, "I know how, but I like to aggravate her a little bit. It's good for her." The two chuckled and then heard, "Well, where are you? I don't want to look at your dining room table."

When the camera turned back around, Colton had the phone. "Hi, Momma. It's me, Colton. I love you so much."

About the Author

Karalee has been writing most of her life, starting with an essay that scored her a near-perfect grade to now publishing books. Her love for words and making them sing the song of stories has become a favorite pastime. She has written about herself, a book of poetry, devotions, and inspirational pages for daily consumption, and now the third book of a series. The series is of a man who first had to find his own way back to God, followed by his experience helping a troubled veteran battling his own demons, continuing on with pulling the veteran and his own family closer together. Her passion for God is in telling stories by using metaphors of real-life situations. Her faith has carried her through some challenging times, and by placing her faith on the pages of her stories, she hopes to bring light to someone's darkened world.